Praise for *Presum*

"Todd Green's *Presumed Guilty* moves us through treacherous terrain in a thoughtful fashion, filled with great stories, and without unnecessary jargon. We learn how to talk about religion and the role it does (and does not) play in terrorism, how to speak with Muslims about terrorism, and how to understand that the larger context of terrorism has nothing to do with Muslims. It is strongly recommended for members of the media, policy makers, and anyone interested in interfaith conversations."

—Omid Safi, director of Duke Islamic Studies Center

"Green's book is essential reading for anyone still asking Muslims to coddle bigots with reassurance. He makes a clear case for why all people should be afforded the assumption of basic human decency."

—Dalia Mogahed, director of research at Institute for Social Policy and Understanding

"Extraordinarily thought-provoking!"

—Thom Hartmann, host of *The Thom Hartmann Program*

"Todd Green offers a nuanced perspective on the history and place of Muslims in America, and a crucial corrective against the rampant and dangerous stereotyping of this group of fellow Americans."
—Jill Jacobs, rabbi and executive director of T'ruah: The Rabbinic Call for Human Rights

"In *Presumed Guilty*, Todd Green slowly and methodically destroys the dangerous myth that Muslim equals terrorist. In its place, Green not only shows us how Islamophobia harms everyone, Muslims and non-Muslims alike, but also offers a guide for building better interfaith understanding. *Presumed Guilty* is timely, necessary, and an incredibly useful book."
—Moustafa Bayoumi, author of *How Does It Feel to Be a Problem? Being Young and Arab in America*

"As Christians, we are called to live out the greatest commandment: to love God and neighbor. In a time of rising Islamophobia and bigotry, this means we must defend our Muslim neighbor against the twin falsehoods that Islam inspires or condones terrorism and that Muslims are solely responsible for its repudiation. As Todd Green demonstrates, all of us—as people of different religions and worldviews—are responsible for condemning oppression, violence, and terrorism as detrimental to human flourishing, just peace, and the well-being of creation."
—Elizabeth A. Eaton, presiding bishop of the Evangelical Lutheran Church in America

"Lucid and personal, scholarly and accessible, Todd Green reminds his readers that the humanity of Muslims comes before the crimes committed in their name by some. The implication that most Muslims are held guilty by association by sections of the media, policy makers, and some governments for the unspeakable terrorist crimes most Muslims deplore is to dehumanize the world's second-largest religious community. *Presumed Guilty* counters the false and damaging narratives of Islamophobia informed by a Christian perspective with clarity and humanity. A must read."
—**Ebrahim Moosa, University of Notre Dame**

"Todd H. Green is a rarity in the academic community: a scholar who can seamlessly weave his academic knowledge together with real-world experience, in prose as clear and lively as a brook. In an age when facts are ignored and experts maligned, *Presumed Guilty* is a book we need now."
—**Carla Power, author of** *If the Oceans Were Ink: An Unlikely Friendship and a Journey to the Heart of the Quran*

Presumed Guilty

Presumed Guilty

Why We Shouldn't Ask Muslims to Condemn Terrorism

Todd H. Green

Foreword by Eboo Patel

Fortress Press
Minneapolis

PRESUMED GUILTY
Why We Shouldn't Ask Muslims to Condemn Terrorism

The opinions and characterizations in this piece are those of the author and do not necessarily reflect the opinions of the US government.

Cover design: Brad Norr

Print ISBN: 978-1-5064-2059-2
eBook ISBN: 978-1-5064-2060-8

The paper used in this publication meets the minimum requirements of American National Standard for Information Sciences — Permanence of Paper for Printed Library Materials, ANSI Z329.48-1984.

Manufactured in the U.S.A.

This book was produced using Pressbooks.com, and PDF rendering was done by PrinceXML.

Contents

Acknowledgments   xi

Foreword   xv
Eboo Patel

Introduction   xxi

PART I. ASSUMING ISLAM IS THE CAUSE OF TERRORISM

1. The True Roots of Terrorism   3

2. Monitoring, Managing, and Maligning Muslims   25

PART II. IGNORING MUSLIMS WHO CONDEMN TERRORISM

3. Muslims Speak Out   49

4. Muslims Take Action   73

PART III. DIVERTING ATTENTION FROM WESTERN VIOLENCE

5. The Sins of the Fathers   99

6. A Written Memorial   119

7. Who Lives, Who Dies, Who Tells Your Story   141

Conclusion: Assuming the Best of Our Muslim Neighbors   163

Suggested Further Reading   181

Index   185

Acknowledgments

The day after the election of Donald J. Trump to the US presidency, I felt overwhelmed. The feeling had less to do with whether my candidate won or lost than with the reality of the blatant key role Islamophobia played in elevating a politician to the most powerful position in the world. Trump's unlikely bid for the White House could not have succeeded without his orchestrated effort to stir up fear and hostility toward Muslims. I've spent the better part of a decade researching and speaking out against Islamophobia, but the 2016 elections made one thing clear. Whatever it was I was doing, it wasn't enough.

This book is an effort to do more, to raise the bar even higher when it comes to how we talk about and to our Muslim neighbors. That said, publishing books calling for understanding and compassion toward Muslims is not for the faint of heart at this moment in our political history. I am grateful to Fortress Press for supporting a project that not only goes against political convention but also promotes a countercultural message.

Thank you to my editor, Lisa Kloskin, who was both accommodating and patient with me in the writing process. Her incisive feedback on manuscript drafts proved invaluable in helping me structure my thoughts and hone my message.

My time as a Franklin Fellow at the State Department in Washington, DC, proved most productive in enabling me to think through how to better communicate with government audiences on the topic of this book. In particular, I appreciated the many opportunities I had in Washington to offer a more constructive framework for engaging Muslim communities that did not depend on troublesome counterterrorism and countering violent extremism models. I want to thank the American Academy of Religion and the Henry Luce Foundation for providing generous funding and support for my year at the State Department. I also want to thank Luther College for its financial and institutional support during my time in Washington.

Several colleagues and friends made helpful comments on drafts of different chapters that have improved the quality of the final product. I'm particularly grateful to Brian Adams, Sophia Arjana, Craig Considine, Rahuldeep Gill, Trina Jones, and Megan Sijapati for such stellar insights and feedback.

A big thanks goes out to my friend Eboo Patel, the founder and director of the Interfaith Youth Core, for writing the foreword. Eboo's tireless efforts to build bridges of interfaith understanding and cooperation have inspired me for years. I am honored to have his wisdom frame the larger message of this book.

Finally, I would be lost in this world without my wife and daughter, Tabita and Rebecka. They are not only exceptional proofreaders, they are the best partners I can imagine. If I have learned anything at all about what it means to be a good neighbor to those who are unjustly marginalized and maligned, I've learned it from them.

Foreword

Eboo Patel

At a rally in Melbourne, Florida, while raising the specter of the dangers posed to the United States by Muslim immigrants, Donald Trump made an ominous statement about "what happened in Sweden last night." The context suggested that he was referring to a terrorist attack committed by a Muslim that the mainstream media had failed to report. The only problem was that nothing much had happened in Sweden the night before. Some people had fun with the blunder by tweeting things like, "Millions are suffering from free healthcare, superb education, well-engineered cars, and awesome meatballs. #PrayForSweden #swedenincident."[1]

Unfortunately, prejudice against an identity group is no laughing matter. "Words create worlds," the great rabbi Abraham Joshua Heschel reminds us. He adds: "What begins in a word ends in a deed."

Speaking in ways that assume Muslims are all somehow responsible for terrorism creates a world in which discriminating against and attacking Muslims is acceptable.

I flew into Kansas City on the night of February 23, 2017, to speak at an interfaith event called "Project Equality" and found a city stunned into silence. The night before, in a bar just outside the city, a white man had hounded two men of Indian descent about their immigration status. Asked to leave because of his belligerence, Adam Purinton returned with a gun and shot both Indian men, killing one. He also shot another man who attempted to intervene. Purinton fled to another bar, where he was captured after boasting to a worker that he had just killed two "Iranian" men.

It took Trump nearly a week to even mention the incident, a fact that deeply disturbed the editorialists at the *Kansas City Star*. They observed, "During such moments of crisis, people look to the president for strength and guidance." Where, the *Star* wondered, was Trump's Twitter finger, lightning fast when it came to highlighting violence committed by dark-skinned immigrants but curiously inert when some members of that group were victims of a crime accompanied by rhetoric that Trump regularly used. People need to hear, the *Star* continued, "the affirmation that the U.S. values everyone's contribution, whether immigrant or native-born."[2]

A democratic society relies on the contributions of its citizens in everything from launching technology companies to joining the PTA. Assuming the worst about an identity group is simple prejudice, and prejudice in a democratic society is not just a violation of a community's dignity, it is a barrier to their contribution. The contributions of Muslims to American civilization are impressive and wide-ranging, captured well in the speech President Barack Obama gave in Cairo on June 4, 2009: "American Muslims have enriched the United States. They have fought in our wars, served in government, stood for civil rights, started businesses, taught at our Universities, excelled in our sports arenas, won Nobel Prizes, built our tallest building, and lit the Olympic Torch."[3]

In his important new book, Todd Green lays out the various reasons that expecting Muslims to condemn terrorism is wrongheaded. In closing this foreword, I want to add one more: the odor of prejudice in the atmosphere does internal damage to identity that is harder to see but is deeply pernicious. The social theorist Charles Taylor points out that identity development is a highly complex and fraught process. Our identities are developed in an ongoing dialogue between our own self-perception and the manners in which we are perceived and represented by others. Taylor writes, "a person or group of people can suffer real damage, real distortion, if the people or society around them mirror back to them a confining or demeaning or contemptible picture of themselves. . . . [M]isrecognition . . . can inflict a grievous wound, saddling its victims with a crippling self-hatred."[4]

I am negotiating this right now as the father of two Muslim boys who wants them to grow up feeling proud of being Muslim and committed to contributing to the various communities to which they belong. Highlighting Muslim artists is one of the ways I do this, so when a band of Muslim musicians from Mali called Tinariwen announced a stop at a local music venue, I excitedly showed my ten-year-old a poster advertising the show. The image depicted smiling men holding musical instruments and dressed in the traditional garb of their local desert region—flowing robes and head wraps. "What are you doing, dad," my son exclaimed. "That's ISIS."

Somehow, a ten-year-old boy—raised in a liberal Muslim household, in a multicultural upper-middle-class neighborhood of Chicago, surrounded by authority figures who know and affirm his Muslim identity, sent to a progressive Muslim religious education program where inspiring stories about Islam make up the curriculum, exposed to a wide range of positive Muslim role models—upon seeing dark men dressed in robes and head wraps, instinctively associates them with terrorists, even though the poster was featured at a concert venue.

Prejudice released into the atmosphere becomes a poison. Sometimes it is evident, and you can point it out. Other times it is imperceptible but works its way into your system and does harm just the same.

October 24, 2017

Notes

1. Rev. Dr. J. Liam Fox (@JmsWmFox), Twitter, February 19, 2017, quoted in Zack Beauchamp, "Trump's Invention of a Swedish Terrorist Attack Was Funny. But It Likely Comes from a Dark Place," Vox, February 19, 2017, https://tinyurl.com/y9y84fek.

2. *Kansas City Star* Editorial Board, "Editorial: Trump's Silence on Deadly Olathe Shooting is Disquieting," *Kansas City Star*, February 27, 2017, https://tinyurl.com/yacyodkn.

3. "Text: Obama's Speech in Cairo," *New York Times*, June 4, 2009, https://tinyurl.com/o4ch3g.

4. Charles Taylor, "The Politics of Recognition," in *Multiculturalism*, ed. Amy Gutmann (Princeton: Princeton University Press, 1994), 25–26.

Introduction

On a lovely spring evening in Spartanburg, South Carolina, I was enjoying a dinner at a downtown restaurant with a handful of faculty members from nearby Wofford College. We were immersed in an energetic conversation that covered considerable intellectual terrain, but the main topic of conversation was Islamophobia. Yes, that may sound like unpleasant dinnertime conversation, but it was the reason I came to Spartanburg. The night before, I gave a talk on campus on the factors fueling the rise in anti-Muslim prejudice in the United States.

About an hour into our dinner conversation, while I was offering some thoughts on what was driving the use of anti-Muslim rhetoric in the ongoing 2016 primaries, I felt a hand grab my left shoulder. The hand began squeezing as hard as it could. A bit disoriented, I swiveled my head and discovered the face of an elderly woman within inches of my own. Her facial expression was livid. Without relaxing her grip on my shoulder, she forced two words through her clenched teeth:

"Shut! Up!" She trembled as she did it, almost as if she was doing everything in her power not to allow her anger and animosity toward me to erupt like a volcano.

I don't recall saying one word in response. I was too stunned. My mind couldn't catch up with what was happening or why. What I do remember is that her husband, who had been at the front of the restaurant paying for their meal, moved quickly in our direction and grabbed his wife by the arm. He pulled her away from me, though not without effort. She clearly didn't want to let go. But he succeeded in steering her to the front of the restaurant and out the door.

This dramatic episode left everyone at my table temporarily speechless, but eventually, we found our voices and our outrage. Beneath our indignation, however, lay a sense of collective embarrassment. For my Wofford friends, their embarrassment reflected frustration that the incident reinforced stereotypes of the South as intolerant and bigoted. My embarrassment stemmed from the fact that I was the one who triggered this woman's behavior. After all, the only reason we were out in public talking about Islamophobia was because of me. Had I limited my dinnertime conversation to the weather or taken a raincheck on the gracious dinner invitation, everyone would have been spared such an unpleasant ordeal.

We learned from our server (who apologized profusely for what happened) that earlier in the evening, this woman had complained about us. She had asked the server to come over to our table to make us stop talking. She and her husband were sitting at a nearby table and overheard our entire conversation. Suffice it to say, they didn't like what they heard. When the server refused the woman's request, the couple demanded to-go boxes for their food and the check. It was on her way out of the restaurant that she decided to take a detour to give us a piece of her mind.

Clearly, we had the wrong conversation in the wrong place. We talked about anti-Muslim hatred and discrimination, and we did it in public. That's all it took to trigger this woman's violent, hateful response.

Critics of Islam such as Bill Maher and Ayaan Hirsi Ali insist many people in the West suffer from political correctness and are too afraid to criticize Islam and Muslims. That's not my experience. It seems like criticizing Islam and disparaging those who practice it is the *only* thing you can do. What you can't do is talk about the injustices and hatred that Muslims must endure. That, it turns out, will get you reprimanded and mildly assaulted in a restaurant. Or it will inspire vicious internet trolls to hound you. Or it will generate hate mail. Or it will trigger efforts to have you fired from your job or maligned in your community. Or it will lead to death threats. I know, because all of this has happened to me. Of course, my Muslim friends who speak out endure this kind of stuff as well, in much higher doses. It's risky to talk about Islamophobia in public.

If we can't talk about the discrimination faced by Muslims or common misconceptions about Islam, then what can we talk about? The only show in town, it would seem, is the story of violence and terrorism. This story dominates news articles, op-ed pieces, and political speeches. The general consensus is that Islam has a violence problem, an epidemic really, and Muslims need to own up to it. They should make amends for all that is wrong in their religion since the only way to explain terrorist attacks carried out by the likes of al-Qaeda or ISIS is to look to their reputed source of inspiration—Islam.

This criticism most often takes the form of asking or demanding that Muslims condemn terrorist attacks. Public figures pounce on Muslims every time an extremist detonates a bomb or drives a truck into a crowd of innocent people. They see their job as calling Muslims to account based on the often unarticulated conviction that Muslims as a whole must be presumed guilty, that Muslims are tacitly complicit in the crimes committed by their co-religionists. If Muslims want to be exonerated in the court of public opinion, they must take to the streets, the airwaves, or social media and assure the rest of us they reject terrorism.

Politicians and journalists across the ideological spectrum frequently make such demands. In a CNN interview, Roger Cohen of the *New York Times* opined that we will never be able to reduce terrorism "until moderate Muslims really speak out—really say, 'This is not our religion.'"[1] Concerned about the deaths of non-Muslims, Sean Hannity at Fox News asked: "Will prominent Muslim leaders denounce and take on groups like ISIS, Hamas, and condemn and also fight against the unthinkable acts of terrorism?"[2] At the United Nations General Assembly, President Obama called on Muslims to "explicitly, forcefully and consistently reject the ideology of organizations like al Qaeda and ISIL."[3] Even Pope Francis has chimed in. During a visit to Turkey, he told President Erdoğan that "it would be beautiful if all Islamic leaders . . . would speak out clearly and condemn [terrorism]."[4]

What many public figures are prone to do is ask variations of the same question: "Why don't Muslims speak out against terrorism?" Of course, it's not always a question. Sometimes, it's a straightforward demand. But even when it is a question, it's a rhetorical one. The answer is supposed to be obvious—Muslims don't speak out. The question really isn't a question but a condemnation.

It's time we stop asking Muslims to condemn terrorism. I have three reasons for making this counterdemand—three reasons that make up the three parts of this book. First, the question wrongly assumes Islam is the driving force behind terrorism. Second, the question ignores the many ways Muslims already condemn terrorism in word and deed. And third, the question diverts attention from the role that unjust violence, including violence carried out within a Christian framework, has played in shaping national identities and destinies in Europe and the United States.

The connective tissue binding these reasons together is the presumption of guilt. Muslims as a whole are presumed guilty because they have failed to reform an inherently violent religion, to atone for the sins of their co-religionists, and to come to terms with their religion's unique history of horrific violence. This presumption of guilt is an exercise in racist scapegoating. It enables us to project our sins of commission and omission onto the Muslim "Other" so that we need not come to terms with our own history of unjust violence or our own complicity in a violent world order.

Let me be clear. I'm not suggesting we stop condemning Muslim extremists who carry out terrorist attacks. Nor am I suggesting Muslims stop condemning terrorism. All of us should condemn terrorism, irrespective of whether the perpetrators are Muslim extremists, white supremacists, Marxist revolutionaries, or our own government. My main point is that it's time to stop singling out Muslims and asking them to condemn terrorism under the assumption they are guilty of harboring terrorist sympathies or promoting a belief system that lends itself to violence. For the reasons indicated above, this line of questioning is riddled with false assumptions and narratives that say more about "us" than "them."

We face a moral dilemma when it comes to the way we talk about Muslims and their relationship to violence. We struggle to abide by that most ancient commandment: "Thou shalt not bear false witness against thy neighbour" (Exodus 20:16).[5] This leaves us with an inescapable moral question: How do we tell truths about our Muslim neighbors? More specifically, how do we tell truths about our Muslim neighbors when it comes to the violence committed in the name of Islam by the likes of al-Qaeda or ISIS? How do we tell truths about our own violent past and present in the process? I'm writing this book because I want to help us wrestle with these moral issues and to raise the bar when it comes to the way we talk about Muslims and terrorism. And by "we," I mean those of us who are not Muslim. It's non-Muslims, particularly those of us who are white and have at least a nominal Christian background, who need to wrestle with these questions the most.

I recognize that all of this comes across as provocative. The taken-for-granted narrative is that when it comes to terrorism, Muslims aren't saying and doing enough. For me to suggest they do even less, or that the moral burden falls on the rest of us when it comes to engaging the topics of Islam and terrorism more honestly and in a more informed way—it all seems a bit much.

To speak about Islam in a responsible manner, to speak honestly about Muslims and ourselves on the topic of violence, is to be provocative. Any story that doesn't confirm preexisting suspicions of violent Muslims at odds with a peaceful West will be deemed provocative. So here it is—a provocative book. Yet a book that provokes can also invite. In the end, that's what I want this book to be—an invitation to raise our standards and to examine our prejudices when it comes to the questions we ask of Muslims and ourselves about violence. Accepting this invitation won't nullify our concerns about terrorism or the threats posed by organizations like ISIS. But it will open the door to asking better questions of our Muslim neighbors, questions based not on the presumption of guilt but on the promise of friendship.

Notes

1. "NYT Columnist: Moderate Muslims Held Responsible Too," video, 1:55, CNN, January 9, 2015, https://tinyurl.com/y7upgaa5.

2. Ellie Sandmeyer and Michelle Leung, "Muslim Leaders Have Roundly Denounced Islamic State, but Conservative Media Won't Tell You That," Media Matters for America, August 21, 2014, https://tinyurl.com/y7zygmep.

3. "Remarks by President Obama in Address to the United Nations General Assembly," The White House, September 24, 2014, https://tinyurl.com/y9b83s57.

4. Philip Pullella, "Pope Says It's Wrong to Equate Islam with Violence," *Reuters*, November 30, 2014, https://tinyurl.com/y7nuj9hu.

5. Unless otherwise stated, citations from biblical texts will use the New Revised Standard Version. In this instance, the citation comes from the King James Version.

PART I

Assuming Islam Is the Cause of Terrorism

1

The True Roots of Terrorism

In the spring of 2017, I participated on a panel hosted by a political organization in Berlin. The theme was media portrayals of Muslims. It didn't take long for the discussion to segue from problematic media narratives about Muslims to anxieties throughout Europe about Muslim extremists. This was to be expected given the Berlin Christmas Market attack that had taken place just five months earlier, not to mention the various attacks that had taken place in the past year or two in Paris, Brussels, and London.

In one memorable exchange, a co-panelist representing the American Jewish Committee took issue with my observation that Islam is not the root cause of terrorism. I had pointed out that many of the perpetrators of terrorist attacks in Europe either had little knowledge of Islam or were not particularly observant in following Islam. Or both.

"That doesn't matter," she responded as she pivoted to the threat terrorism posed to Jews in particular. "The perpetrators are Muslims. We must take that seriously. After all, *Muslims are targeting Jews in Europe. Muslims are killing Jews.*" She was referring to the January 2015 terrorist attack on a kosher grocery store in Paris in which an ISIS supporter killed four Jewish hostages. "This *is* about Islam."

I agreed with the larger point she was trying to make. Many Jews in Europe feel less safe not only due to terrorist attacks like the one in Paris but also because of the anti-Semitism that exists in some Muslim communities. These are legitimate concerns. But I took issue with how she framed the problem of terrorism as fundamentally an Islamic one. "If Islam is the cause of terrorist attacks in places like Paris or Berlin," I insisted, "then Islam is also the cause of the 'non-terrorism' that exists among the overwhelming majority of Muslims throughout Europe and indeed the world. Blaming Islam gets us nowhere since most Muslims aren't terrorists. If we are ever going to understand terrorism, we must look to factors beyond Islam."

My co-panelist was not alone in viewing Islam as the cause of terrorism. Framing terrorism as Islamic is pervasive in political discourse. Donald Trump insisted ad nauseam during his presidential campaign that those who refuse to say "radical Islamic terrorism" suffer from political correctness. If we are going to defeat terrorism, according to Trump, we must be willing to use these three magical words, with an emphasis on "Islamic." His rhetoric resonated not only with the GOP platform but with many voters.

This framing is also widespread in popular culture. Consider one of Islam's most prominent critics, the best-selling author Ayaan Hirsi Ali. In her book *Heretic*, she writes: "Islamic violence is rooted not in social, economic, or political conditions—or even in theological error—but rather in the foundational texts of Islam itself."[1] Hirsi Ali sees Islam as existing in some sort of vacuum. One need not bother with understanding how historical, social, or political factors affect the ways in which Muslims read or interpret their foundational texts, whether in terms of violence or peace. Islam is violent by nature.

Or take the well-respected journalist Graeme Wood. In March 2015, he penned an article for *The Atlantic* titled "What ISIS Really Wants."[2] In it, he claims "the reality is that the Islamic State is Islamic. *Very* Islamic." Wood's argument about the Islamic nature of ISIS found receptive audiences across the political spectrum. Many religion scholars, however, expressed disappointment in the piece, not so much because it situated ISIS within an Islamic framework but because it elevated religious ideology as the key lens through which to understand the organization. Wood, like Trump and Hirsi Ali, paid little attention to the political and social conditions driving ISIS's particular interpretations of Islam.

This brings us back to examining the logic behind referring to terrorism as "Islamic." If Trump, Hirsi Ali, and Wood are right, if an organization such as ISIS is Islamic, then so are the more than one billion Muslims who abhor ISIS. Insisting that ISIS is Islamic tells us nothing about why a small minority of Muslims are drawn to the terrorist organization and its extreme ideology while most are not. If we are going to understand terrorism, we must stop making assumptions and start looking to sound scholarship and reputable data. When we do so, we discover a body of evidence that debunks any organic link between Islam and terrorism.

What Drives Terrorism

Scholarly opinions differ widely on how best to explain why people become terrorists and on how religion factors into the so-called radicalization process. But there is a general consensus among scholars and experts that terrorism is not primarily fueled by religion.

Politics matters more than religion. The political scientist Robert Pape has compiled a database of every suicide attack in the world since 1980. What he found is that of all the suicide attacks that occurred between 1980 and 2003, 95 percent of them had one thing in common, and it wasn't Islam or even religion. It was foreign military occupation.[3] Suicide attackers and the organizations they belong to are attempting to assert political self-determination by force against real or perceived occupying powers. They want to compel democratic governments to withdraw from land or territory that they have some sort of claim on.

Suicide attackers can be Muslim, but Pape found that half of suicide attacks were carried out by people with secular worldviews.[4] This includes groups such as the Tamil Tigers in Sri Lanka, an organization with a Marxist orientation that is opposed to religion. In the time period covered, the Tamil

Tigers carried out more suicide attacks than Hamas, a Muslim resistance organization in Palestine.[5]

Whether suicide attackers are religious or secular, the goal behind their efforts is almost always the same: the removal of occupying forces. Pape's observations are supported by statements made by many terrorist groups. Hezbollah, a Shi'a militant organization in Lebanon, declared in its "Open Letter" in 1985 that its main purpose was "to put an end to foreign occupation." This included efforts "to expel the Americans, the French and their allies from Lebanon, putting an end to any colonialist entity on our land."[6]

In the case of al-Qaeda, Osama bin Laden stated in 1998: "The call to wage war against America was made because America . . . [is] sending tens of thousands of its troops to the land of the two Holy Mosques over and above its meddling in its affairs and its politics."[7] Concerning why al-Qaeda attacked the United States on 9/11, bin Laden pointed out in 2004 that this decision was made only "after it became unbearable and we witnessed the oppression and tyranny of the American/Israeli coalition against our people in Palestine and Lebanon."[8]

Even in more recent cases such as ISIS, Pape notes the role of occupation and loss of territory in suicide attacks. ISIS-inspired attacks in Belgium and France are, in part, responses to military campaigns by these countries that have contributed to territorial losses. ISIS has also employed suicide attacks in battles in Iraq in an effort to take hold of or retain territory against opposing forces.[9]

Pape doesn't ignore the role of religion. "Religion is rarely the root cause," he argues, "although it is often used as a tool by terrorist organizations in recruiting."[10] To put it another way, religion helps to validate the larger political goal of suicide attacks, but it is not the driving force behind the attacks. His views echo those of many prominent scholars who see politics as the catalyst and religion as the legitimizer of terrorism.[11]

Other scholars prefer to highlight social factors more than political ones. Scott Atran, an anthropologist, argues that terrorism is driven to a large extent by individuals in search not only of a cause but of a sense of family and kinship with others. He calls it the "band of brothers" theory. Based on fieldwork and interviews with a variety of extremists, from Muslim *mujahideen* (holy warriors) to ISIS soldiers, Atran believes that terrorists "don't simply kill and die for a cause. They kill and die for each other."[12] The brotherly and familial bonds forged between jihadists through social networks are key to understanding what makes someone willing to turn to terrorism.

Many of the people who join terrorist organizations and carry out attacks often do so through relationships built with classmates, teammates, coworkers, or other family members. An illustration of this dynamic can be seen with three of the 9/11 pilots: Marwan al-Shehhi, Mohamed Atta, and Ziad Jarrah. These three, along with the so-called "twentieth hijacker," Ramzi bin al-Shibh, became good friends as university students in Hamburg. They developed deep connections with one another, meeting and talking at length in dorms, fast-food restaurants, libraries, and halal butcher shops. Al-Qaeda didn't recruit these four men. They radicalized one another first, and only then did they seek out a larger cause for which they were willing to fight. Al-Qaeda provided them with that cause.

The Hamburg cell developed as these four men interacted and socialized with one another in person. Increasingly, however, the internet and social media are helping disillusioned young people in search of a brotherhood and a cause to find kindred spirits virtually. Much of ISIS's recruitment in Europe, for example, depends heavily on forging relationships through digital platforms with and between disillusioned young Muslims.[13] In some instances, these ISIS recruits attempt to travel to Syria and Iraq to translate their virtual relationships into flesh-and-blood ones. In other instances, the relationships they have forged with ISIS recruiters will remain in the digital realm, and their terrorist activity will be directed toward domestic targets. But the same factors are still driving these behaviors—a cause to fight for that is discovered within a social network. Preexisting family or friendship bonds continue to be key to ISIS recruitment. More than three out of every four individuals who join ISIS from abroad do so in conjunction with family or friends.[14]

Other motivations play a role in who becomes a would-be terrorist, including the search for grandeur, adventure, and acceptance from peers. Religion is important too, though not as a catalyst. Religious ideologies and obligations convey sacredness to a cause. Terrorists can and often do appeal to Islamic texts and teachings as they invoke divine rewards or punishment for their actions. Islam can sustain their commitment to a cause, but it's not the source of their inspiration.[15] Terrorists will not shed blood and make the ultimate sacrifice for abstract religious ideologies. They will do so with and for a "band of brothers" in the service of a glorious mission.

Marc Sageman, a forensic psychiatrist and former CIA operations officer, believes a combination of social and political factors best explain terrorism and the rise of groups such as ISIS. He develops a theory quite similar to Atran's "band of brothers." For Sageman, Islamist terrorism arises organically from the bottom up when "bunches of guys"—trusted friends, childhood pals, or close relatives—make a collective decision to connect with a terrorist organization.[16] It's the network, the group, that is key to understanding how individuals are mobilized along the path toward terrorism.

Individuals often start down this path by experiencing a sense of moral outrage at the suffering of other Muslims. When this outrage resonates with their own personal experiences or frustrations and is then amplified within a group, the pieces are in place for these individuals to move down the path of radicalization.[17]

Sageman believes we must also understand the political circumstances that give rise to terrorist organizations and create the conditions that evoke moral outrage. In the case of ISIS, the US invasion of Iraq and the mass slaughter of Sunni

Muslims is what led to this brutal organization. For many who join ISIS, they are connecting their moral outrage to tragedies that took place because of overtly political and military decisions.[18]

ISIS, in turn, advances its own political agenda in Syria and Iraq to counter perceived Western occupation and to avenge past injustices such as torture and mass killing. This is where religion comes into the equation—playing a role as justifier. ISIS uses Islam to promote and legitimize its political agenda, not vice versa. Islam also serves as a vehicle for moral outrage and a conveyer of identity for those seeking a larger purpose with the caliphate. But Islam is neither the cause of ISIS-related terrorism nor the reason people join ISIS.[19]

Pape, Atran, and Sageman aren't the only experts on terrorism, but they are among the most prominent in the field. They have advised government agencies, high-level policymakers, military leaders, and the United Nations. Their insights have much to teach us about how to talk about and make sense of terrorism. All three draw conclusions based on data gathered from extensive research of real-world events and, in some instances, interviews with terrorists. All reject explanatory models outlining a clear, cookie-cutter pathway toward radicalization to violence that makes it possible to predict who will become a terrorist. Most importantly, all believe Islam is instrumentalized by groups such as ISIS and al-Qaeda to justify or sanctify their cause, but they reject the assumption that Islamic ideology is the catalyst of terrorism.

Religion plays a part, but political and social factors are the key to making sense of why terrorists do what they do.

Religiously Illiterate Terrorists

I once gave a lecture at the FBI Academy to a gathering of prominent law enforcement officials that provided an overview of the above scholarship. As I finished my presentation and opened the floor to questions, one police officer responded incredulously: "All of this sounds like wishful thinking. I mean, c'mon, these guys are shouting 'Allahu Akbar' right before they blow themselves up. They've gotta be doing this because of Islam, right?"

He had a point. A terrorist who cries "Allahu Akbar" at the very least is claiming Islam as a motivation. We must take that seriously. Yet, how much do we really learn about the religious convictions of someone who shouts this phrase? What can we conclude about his knowledge of Islam? His familiarity with Islamic texts and traditions? His level of commitment or practice? The answer to all of these questions is the same. Not much. In fact, the evidence we have about Muslim terrorists suggests they know very little about the religion they are claiming as a source of inspiration.

In a classified study by the Behavioural Science Unit of MI5, Britain's domestic counterintelligence agency, researchers found religious illiteracy to be quite high among those engaged in violent extremist behavior. Most were novices when it came to Islam, while many others were not observant in their faith. Some drank alcohol, called on prostitutes, and took drugs—all behaviors shunned in traditional Islam. Far from viewing Islam as the cause of terrorism, MI5 concluded that a more deeply cultivated engagement with Islam can shield individuals who otherwise might be drawn to violent extremism.[20]

When interviewing imprisoned ISIS fighters in Iraq, the Oxford scholar Lydia Wilson discovered many of them had very little knowledge of Islam. "They are woefully ignorant about Islam," she explains, "and have difficulty answering questions about Sharia law, militant jihad, and the caliphate." Anger over American occupation after the Iraq War, and the promise of defending their identity as Iraqi Sunni Arabs, led many of these imprisoned fighters to ISIS, not Islamic theology.[21] Her findings match those of a study conducted by the United Nations Office of Counter-Terrorism, which found that young men who leave their homes in Europe or the Middle East to fight for terrorist groups lack a basic understanding of Islam.[22]

Didier François, a French journalist, discovered all of this the hard way—as an ISIS prisoner. During his ten-month captivity in Syria, François had plenty of opportunities to talk with his captors, but they steered clear of any theological debates. "There was never really discussion about texts or—it was not a religious discussion," noted François in an interview with CNN after his release. They were interested in politics, not religion. He added: "It was more hammering what they were believing than teaching us about the Quran. Because it has nothing to do with the Quran."[23]

ISIS's own recruiting forms, leaked to the media in 2016, reveal how little ISIS recruits know about Islam. According to information analyzed from just over three thousand of these documents, 70 percent of recruits acknowledged possessing little knowledge of Sharia. Another 24 percent had an intermediate knowledge, while only 5 percent claimed advanced expertise.[24] What these documents reveal is that religious illiteracy is not the exception but the norm among ISIS recruits. In fact, it appears that ISIS preys on this illiteracy to attract people to its ranks, presumably because ill-informed recruits are easier to persuade and manipulate than those well-versed in Islamic texts and traditions.

You don't have to scour through leaked MI5 or ISIS documents or interview ISIS soldiers to learn that many terrorists have little familiarity with Islam. If you pay close attention to the news, you will find plenty of examples of Islam-ignorant extremists. My favorite story involves two young men from Birmingham, England: Yusuf Sarwar and Mohammed Ahmed. Before heading off to Syria to wage violent jihad, the two childhood buddies went on Amazon to find some books that would help them prepare the fight. What did they end up ordering? *Islam for Dummies* and *The Koran for Dummies*.[25] That's right. Two men who had *already* made the decision to travel to Syria and join a terrorist organization ordered Dummies books on Islam so that they could learn about the faith for which they were willing to die.

If Islam were the main source of inspiration for Muslim terrorists, we would not expect them to order books like *Islam for Dummies*, nor would we expect the degree of religious illiteracy that we have encountered in the studies and stories described here. Islamic ideology may be the politically popular explanation for terrorism, but it's not an explanation supported by the evidence. When it comes to Islam, the behavior of Muslim terrorists has much more to do with ignorance than ideology.

How Responsible Are Muslims for Terrorists Attacks?

Since 9/11, the word "terrorist" has become synonymous with "Muslim." If CNN or the BBC has breaking news about a terrorist attack, many of us assume the story is about Muslims behaving badly. We've become accustomed to the idea that Muslims have a monopoly on terrorism.

Except they don't. Not by a long shot. The data collected on terrorist attacks in the United States and Europe points overwhelmingly to a little-known or acknowledged fact. Most terrorist attacks are perpetrated by non-Muslims.

According to the FBI, between 1980 and 2005, 94 percent of terrorist attacks on US soil were carried out by non-Muslims.[26] We should keep in mind that this data includes the 9/11 attacks. Of course, the issue is more complicated than doing a simple headcount. Although Muslims carried out a very small portion of attacks, it doesn't take many people to do considerable damage, as we saw on 9/11. But this point holds for non-Muslim terrorists as well, such as Timothy McVeigh's attack on the Alfred P. Murrah Federal Building in Oklahoma City in 1995.

If we examine the data on violent deaths in the United States, we also discover that Muslim extremists are not the primary culprits. According to the Triangle Center on Terrorism and Homeland Security, from just after 9/11 through 2015, Muslim extremists killed sixty-nine people. Yet in that same period, more than 220,000 Americans were murdered.[27] If we assume that people killed in terrorist attacks by Muslims are also victims of murder, then it's clear that murders committed by Muslim extremists pale in comparison to the number of murders carried out by others.

The Triangle Center also noted that in 2015 alone, 134 Americans were killed in mass shootings.[28] That means the number of people killed in mass shootings over a one-year period is nearly twice the number of people killed by Muslim extremists over a fourteen-year period. And yet mass shootings don't receive nearly the amount of attention or concern from politicians as terrorist attacks carried out by Muslims. Focusing incessantly on a "Muslim threat" pays greater political dividends than trying to address mass shootings carried out by violent white men.

Even if we don't concern ourselves with mass shootings or murders more generally but keep our focus on terrorist attacks, the greatest threat does not lie with Muslim extremists. According to the Combating Terrorism Center (CTC) at the US Military Academy, it lies with right-wing extremists. In the decade after 9/11, right-wing extremists carried out 337 attacks and killed 254 people.[29] Since 9/11, right-wing extremists have been far deadlier on average than Muslim extremists.

Law enforcement agencies agree that it's not Muslim extremists who pose the greatest terrorist danger. The Triangle Center conducted a survey of law enforcement agencies from around the country in 2014. Of the 382 agencies surveyed, 74 percent indicated that anti-government extremism is among the top three terrorist threats in their jurisdiction. Only 39 percent reported al-Qaeda or similar terrorist organizations as one of their top three terrorist threats. Local police agencies are in the best position to know what's happening in their own jurisdictions when it comes to the activities of extremist groups. If they are pointing the finger at anti-government extremists, we should take that seriously.

This recognition of the threat of right-wing extremists, including that posed by anti-government activists and white supremacists, made its way to Capitol Hill in September 2017. During a hearing with FBI director Chris Wray, Claire McCaskill, a member of the Senate Homeland Security and Government Affairs Committee, remarked that the greater attention given to ISIS-inspired attacks by the FBI and US government doesn't match what we know about actual terrorist attacks on domestic soil. McCaskill pointed out that the number of white supremacist and anti-government attacks were "almost triple" those carried out by individuals connected to international terrorist organizations such as ISIS. Yet white supremacy receives scant attention. "We have had zero hearings on the threat of domestic terrorists and the threat they pose and our response to it," McCaskill insisted, noting that there has been no shortage of hearings on ISIS.[30] The implications of her statements were clear. The federal government focuses much more on ISIS than white supremacy because of politics. It has little to do with the facts on the ground.

In Europe, terrorist attacks by Muslim extremists have been on the rise in the past several years. ISIS has much to do with that. Even so, much of the data from recent decades indicates Muslim extremists are not responsible for the majority of attacks. According to Europol, between 2009 and 2013, less than 2 percent of terrorist attacks in EU countries were deemed "religiously motivated."[31] To take just one of these years, in 2010, there were 249 terrorist attacks in the EU. Europol labeled only three of them as "Islamist" in nature.[32] Most attacks were carried out by individuals or organizations motivated by separatist beliefs or ethno-nationalist fervor. This holds true even for the years after 2013.

To be fair, the number of attacks by Muslim extremists has been on the rise, and the death toll in recent years from these attacks is concerning. In 2016, 135 people were killed in 13 different attacks by Muslim extremists in the EU.[33] Muslim extremists may not carry out the majority of attacks, but depending on the year, they may be responsible for more deaths. This can be explained in part because organizations such as ISIS aim for mass casualties. That's not always the case with attacks carried out by separatist organizations.

The trend in Europe when it comes to attacks from Muslim

extremists is disturbing. There's no denying it. But we must be careful not to assume that this is because Muslims in Europe are more prone to terrorism. Such an assumption flies in the face not only of some of the data discussed above but of the modern history of terrorism in Europe.

If we examine casualties from terrorist attacks in Europe going back to 1970, we discover that until 2004, very few people were killed by Muslim extremists. This is noteworthy because plenty of Muslims have been living in Europe throughout the period in question. But Europe didn't have a problem with Muslim extremists until after the 9/11 attacks. Military campaigns from European countries during and after the War on Terror combined with increased anti-Muslim discrimination and racism have had much to do with the changing dynamics.

This wasn't the case in the 1970s and 1980s, when political tensions and violence in Europe derived not from frustration over wars in Muslim-majority countries but from efforts by organizations to establish some sort of national identity or sovereignty. The Irish Republican Army and the Basque separatist movement *Euskadi Ta Askatasuna* (ETA) were among the organizations wreaking havoc in Europe at the time.

The death toll from terrorist attacks in Europe in the 1970s and 1980s was much greater than what we've seen in Europe since 2004. According to the Global Terrorism Database, in three particular years—1972, 1974, 1980—the casualties exceeded four hundred for the year, with Muslim extremists responsible for only a handful of deaths in 1980 and none in the other two years. The death toll exceeded two hundred in ten of the years between 1970 and 1990, again with Muslim extremists responsible for relatively few deaths. By contrast, the year since 9/11 with the highest death toll from terrorism, 2004, witnessed slightly less than two hundred casualties, most of these coming from the Madrid train bombings.[34]

* * *

None of this is an effort to diminish the deaths of those killed by Muslim extremists. I'm simply providing some historical context. For the better part of three decades since 1970, Muslim extremists had little to do with the terrorist attacks that killed so many in Europe. If we are seeing a change in that trend now, it cannot be because Islam makes Muslims more prone to violence than non-Muslim Europeans. If that were the case, we would have seen more terrorism from individuals with a Muslim background in the 1970s and 1980s. We must look to larger political and social factors if we are to make sense of the recent trends in terrorism in Europe.

The same holds true for terrorism writ large. There's nothing inherent to Islam that leads people to become terrorists. The small number of Muslims who engage in terrorism often lack a basic understanding of Islam. What they do possess is disillusionment, a desire for glory often connected to a political cause, and a yearning for a network or family of sorts with whom to fight and die for this cause. The sooner we recognize this and let go of the habit of blaming Islam for terrorism, the sooner we will be able to make real progress in the battle against terrorism.

Notes

1. Ayaan Hirsi Ali, *Heretic: Why Islam Needs a Reformation Now* (New York: Harper, 2015), 3.

2. Graeme Wood, "What ISIS Really Wants," *The Atlantic*, March 2015, https://tinyurl.com/mb5os8d.

3. Robert Pape, *Dying to Win: The Strategic Logic of Suicide Terrorism* (New York: Random House, 2005), 4.

4. Elliott Balch, "Myth Busting: Robert Pape on ISIS, Suicide Terrorism, and U.S. Foreign Policy," *Chicago Policy Review*, May 5, 2015, https://tinyurl.com/yd93ozx4.

5. Pape, *Dying to Win*, 4.

6. Pape, *Dying to Win*, 31.

7. Pape, *Dying to Win*, 119.

8. "Full Transcript of bin Laden's Speech," *Al Jazeera*, November 1, 2004, https://tinyurl.com/y8xxvlrg.

9. Uri Friedman, "The 'Strategic Logic' of Suicide Bombing," *The Atlantic*, March 23, 2016, https://tinyurl.com/yazzxzgn.

10. Pape, *Dying to Win*, 4.

11. For example, see Jessica Stern and J. M. Berger, *ISIS: The State of Terror* (New York: Ecco, 2015); John Horgan, *Walking Away from Terrorism: Accounts of Disengagement from Radical and Extremist Movements* (New York: Routledge, 2009); Donatella della Porta, *Social Movement Studies and Political Violence* (Aarhus, Denmark: Centre for Studies in Islamism and Radicalisation, 2009); Arun Kundnani, *The Muslims Are Coming! Islamophobia, Extremism, and the Domestic War on Terror* (London: Verso, 2014).

12. Scott Atran, *Talking to the Enemy: Faith, Brotherhood, and the (Un)making of Terrorists* (New York: Ecco, 2010), xi.

13. Bruce Bower, "New Studies Explore Why Ordinary People Turn

Terrorist," *Science News*, June 23, 2016, https://tinyurl.com/yabnz45w.

14. Scott Atran, "Mindless Terrorists? The Truth about ISIS Is Much Worse," *The Guardian*, November 15, 2015, https://tinyurl.com/y89w3dzk.

15. Atran, *Talking to the Enemy*, 37; Atran, "Mindless Terrorists?"

16. Marc Sageman, *Leaderless Jihad: Terror Networks in the Twenty-First Century* (Philadelphia: University of Pennsylvania Press, 2008), 66–69.

17. Sageman, *Leaderless Jihad*, viii, 75.

18. Mehdi Hasan, "How Islamic Is Islamic State?," *New Statesman*, March 10, 2015, https://tinyurl.com/ya2vl57r.

19. Hasan, "How Islamic Is Islamic State?"

20. Alan Travis, "MI5 Report Challenges Views on Terrorism in Britain," *The Guardian*, August 20, 2008, https://tinyurl.com/y8cuqjpf.

21. Lydia Wilson, "What I Discovered from Interviewing Imprisoned ISIS Fighters," *The Nation*, October 21, 2015, https://tinyurl.com/yaan8cog.

22. Lizzie Dearden, "Isis: UN Study Finds Foreign Fighters in Syria 'Lack Basic Understanding of Islam,'" *The Independent*, August 4, 2017, https://tinyurl.com/y7rpdhjr.

23. Mick Krever, "ISIS Captors Cared Little about Religion, Says Former Hostage," CNN, February 4, 2015, https://tinyurl.com/yc3o3to8.

24. Aya Batrawy, Paisley Dodds, and Lori Hinnant, "Leaked ISIS Documents Reveal Recruits Have Poor Grasp of Islamic Faith," *The Independent*, August 16, 2016, https://tinyurl.com/ybkux68s.

25. Vikram Dodd, "Two British Men Admit to Linking Up with Extremist Group in Syria," *The Guardian*, July 8, 2014, https://tinyurl.com/ybbk6cxb.

26. Federal Bureau of Investigation, Counterterrorism Division, *Terrorism 2002–2005*, 57–66, PDF, https://tinyurl.com/y74kmt8d.

27. Charles Kurzman, "Muslim-American Involvement with Violent Extremism, 2015," Triangle Center on Terrorism and Homeland Security, February 2, 2016, 2, PDF, https://tinyurl.com/y8g7shvs.

28. Kurzman, "Muslim-American Involvement with Violent Extremism, 2015."

29. Arie Perliger, *Challengers from the Sidelines: Understanding America's Violent Far-Right*, The Combating Terrorism Center at West Point, November 2012, 100, PDF, https://tinyurl.com/yb2t5zv7.

30. Tara John, "FBI Chief: Agency Has 1,000 Open Domestic Terrorism Investigations," *Time*, September 28, 2017, https://tinyurl.com/y7ccwuxa.

31. For the collection of annual Europol reports on terrorism in the EU, see "EU Terrorism Situation and Trend Report (TE-SAT)," Europol, https://tinyurl.com/kggtzue. For a summary of key findings from the reports between 2009–2013, see Beenish Ahmed, "Less Than 2 Percent of Terrorist Attacks in the E.U. Are Religiously Motivated," ThinkProgress, January 8, 2015, https://tinyurl.com/y7djpujm.

32. "TE–SAT 2011: EU Terrorism Situation and Trend Report," Europol, 2011, 15, PDF, https://tinyurl.com/y78snwar.

33. "EU Terrorism Situation and Trend Report (TE-SAT) 2017," Europol, 2017, 22, PDF, https://tinyurl.com/y9kau2ze.

34. "People Killed by Terrorism per Year in Western Europe 1970–2015," Datagraver, March 22, 2016, https://tinyurl.com/y9ajo3gm.

2

Monitoring, Managing, and Maligning Muslims

In December 2015, concerned students, staff, and faculty at Luther College, a liberal arts college tucked away in the bluffs of northeast Iowa, came together to write a statement of solidarity with Muslims. In the statement, we repudiated the hatred and hostility aimed at Muslims on and beyond our campus. We pledged to build relationships with our Muslim neighbors based on friendship, not fear.[1] It was a significant moment in the history of the college, particularly since ours was not a community with a strong history of activism.

We issued the statement in the midst of a primary race in which candidates increasingly deployed anti-Muslim rhetoric and proposals to drum up support for presidential bids. Presidential contenders and political pundits called for mosque closings, registration systems, ID cards, internment camps, and the halting of refugee resettlement—all targeting

Muslims. We coincidentally published the statement on the same day that Donald Trump demanded "a total and complete shutdown" of Muslims entering the country.[2] We couldn't remain silent in such a hostile political environment, not least of which because many of the candidates stirring up resentment against Muslims were planning to visit our small college town in the buildup to the Iowa caucuses.

The statement not only garnered lots of online signatures and endorsements. It also went viral and was read from coast to coast. Some universities developed solidarity statements modeled on ours. Interfaith organizations and faith communities reached out to the college and expressed gratitude for our leadership. It's not often that a liberal arts college in a small corner of Iowa contributes to a national conversation about the importance of affirming religious pluralism and rejecting religious bigotry.

Dissenters on campus were in the minority, but some did make their voice heard. One young man, a sophomore, wrote a letter to the college newspaper taking us to task for the statement. "The issue of Islamophobia is not some grand fight against oppression and evil," he assured us.[3]

"I could not disagree more," I responded in my own letter. "Islamophobia is a systemic prejudice that has horrific implications for Muslims or those perceived to be Muslim (Arabs, Sikhs, etc.)." I reminded him that Islamophobia has led to registration programs, surveillance and profiling by law enforcement and intelligence agencies, and detentions and deportations. In its more violent forms, Islamophobia has resulted in hate crimes, torture, and murder. "Whatever else the fight against Islamophobia is, it's definitely a 'grand fight against oppression.'"[4]

The young man did not have ill intent. He simply had not given Islamophobia much thought. Understandable. After all, he was white and Christian in a nation in which white, male Christians have always held positions of power and privilege. He's never been treated as a terrorist suspect. He's never been told to go back to his own country. He's never had to worry whether the church or the café he frequents is under surveillance. Islamophobia wasn't something he had experienced firsthand.

Muslims don't have the luxury of debating whether Islamophobia is oppressive. Anti-Muslim prejudice constitutes a lived experience for them, a daily reality from which there is no escape. Politics and policies frame Muslims as terrorist suspects and national security threats, under the assumption Islam itself is inherently violent and Muslims by default are guilty of terrorist tendencies. That's why Muslims must be managed, registered, and surveilled, or worse.

Registration Programs

Trump's flirtations with a Muslim database during his presidential campaign attracted both enthusiastic praise and swift condemnations. But the idea was hardly new. The United States already experimented with one Muslim registration program. In the immediate aftermath of 9/11, the Bush administration implemented the National Security

Entry-Exit Registration System (NSEERS) under the oversight of the Department of Homeland Security (DHS) in 2002. NSEERS required men with temporary visas entering the United States from twenty-five countries, all but one Muslim-majority, to register with the United States government. Tens of thousands of Muslim men entering the country were interviewed, fingerprinted, and photographed as part of the registration.

Human rights and civil liberties organizations, from the American-Arab Anti-Discrimination Committee to the American Civil Liberties Union, condemned the racial and religious profiling undergirding NSEERS. Their concerns were understandable given that evidence of criminal or violent behavior was not a prerequisite for registration. The program clearly assumed that Muslim men were suspect persons possessing terrorist inclinations.

The DHS suspended portions of NSEERS in 2011, stating that the registration procedures previously in place for nonimmigrant travelers "no longer provides any increase in security" in light of updated automated systems that collected arrival and exit information more efficiently.[5] The Obama administration dismantled the program more thoroughly in December 2016, just one month before Trump took office.

NSEERS yielded zero terrorism convictions yet cost an estimated $10 million dollars per year at its peak. The Office of the Inspector General at the DHS acknowledged that this money was not well spent. It also noted that tracking and interrogating individuals based on their background in Arab or Muslim-majority countries was an ineffective way of preventing terrorist attacks.[6]

Profiling and Surveillance

In both the United States and Europe, a wave of counterterrorism measures after 9/11 resulted in Muslim communities becoming subject to intense profiling and surveillance from law enforcement and intelligence agencies. The impetus for such actions arose from the Bush administration's War on Terror. Counterterrorism at this time focused almost exclusively on Muslims. During the Obama years, the United States government expanded the scope of counterterrorism policies, at least in theory, to include other forms of violent extremist ideologies and organizations. It also supplemented "hard" approaches to fighting terrorism—surveillance, profiling, the use of force—with supposedly "soft" approaches that focused on preventing at-risk individuals from becoming attracted to terrorist ideas and activity. This latter approach became known as Countering Violent Extremism (CVE). In practice, both approaches in the Obama administration continued to target Muslim communities disproportionately and to depend heavily on religious and racial profiling.

The Obama administration found inspiration for some of its CVE initiatives from Britain's Preventing Violent Extremism program, or Prevent for short. Prevent launched the year after the 2005 London bombings that killed fifty-six people and injured almost eight hundred. The idea behind Prevent was to supplement counterterrorism work with efforts to prevent individuals from becoming radicalized. The British government partnered with Muslim organizations and leaders deemed "moderate" in the hopes of countering the ideologies that presumably were the root cause of terrorism. The government poured hundreds of millions of pounds into after-school programs, sports leagues, language classes, and mosque renovations, all with the intent of integrating Muslims into mainstream society and drawing them away from radical ideas.[7]

On both sides of the Atlantic, counterterrorism and CVE programs depended on deeply flawed radicalization theories. Law enforcement and intelligence agencies developed these theories as a means to predict who was likely to engage in terrorist activities. A prominent example can be found in the NYPD's 2007 report, *Radicalization in the West: The Homegrown Threat*. The report lays out four stages of radicalization: preradicalization, self-identification, indoctrination, and jihadization. As Muslims, particularly young men, move through these consecutive stages, they become increasingly devout. For example, they may grow a beard or stop drinking or gambling. Such religious behaviors, in the NYPD radicalization paradigm, constitute suspicious activities suggesting a path toward radicalization. The more "Muslim" one behaves, the more likely that person will turn into a violent jihadist. To put it another way, a Muslim who pursues the straight and narrow is treated very differently than a white born-again Christian who does the same. A sober Muslim is deemed a security risk; a sober Christian is not.

Counterterrorism and CVE programs, along with the radicalization theories that undergirded them, paved the way for extensive surveillance and profiling of Muslim communities. In the United States, the NYPD implemented an extensive surveillance program of Muslim communities after 9/11. A secret division known as the Demographics Unit monitored and spied on Muslims, relying on Muslim "mosque-crawlers" to infiltrate mosques. This program came under fire from civil liberties and human rights organizations for its overdependence on religious and racial profiling. In 2014, the program disbanded. The chief of the NYPD intelligence division admitted that the program had not produced one criminal lead since its inception.[8]

The FBI has made extensive use of Muslim informants and agents provocateurs in an effort to infiltrate Muslim communities and to incite members of these communities to engage in terrorism. The idea is to head off terrorism before it materializes, a goal that fits into the FBI's larger shift toward terrorism prevention after the 9/11 attacks.[9] But the FBI's use of Muslim informants is fraught with ethical problems. For example, when FBI informant Shahed Hussain enticed four men from Newburgh, New York, into a plot to bomb two synagogues in 2009, all four were charged and found guilty. But no such plot existed until Hussain created it. Hussain also preyed on the vulnerabilities of the men—one had a mental illness, another had a brother in need of a liver transplant. Hussain used financial incentives to lure these men into the plot. Tactics such as this presuppose that Muslims are guilty of terrorism, and it's the FBI's job to get them to activate their latent terrorist tendencies.[10] It's no wonder why organizations such as Human Rights Watch have condemned the FBI informant program of committing egregious human rights violations, including entrapment and obtaining evidence by coercion.[11]

Britain's domestic intelligence agency, MI5, also employs Muslim informants to gather intelligence on their coreligionists. Some reports suggest informants receive up to £2,000 (approximately $2,600) for the information they provide, though this pales in comparison to the reported $100,000 that Hussain received for his work in Newburgh.[12]

CAGE, a civil liberties organization, has expressed concern about the use of informants and US-style entrapment techniques in Britain. CAGE has also accused the British government more broadly of engaging in "cradle-to-grave" surveillance of Muslim communities. It has noted how Prevent drafts people from educational and caretaking occupations, including teachers and doctors, into the surveillance state and turns them into de facto informants.[13] CAGE is not alone in this complaint. The National Union of Teachers (NUT) voted overwhelmingly to reject the government's Prevent strategy in 2016 on the grounds that it pressured teachers to function as spies and informants. The NUT felt that effective teaching depended on trust between teachers and students, something the Prevent strategy undermined.[14]

Other European countries engage in extensive surveillance of Muslim communities in the name of counterterrorism.

France is the most notable example. It expanded surveillance laws and state emergency powers after the *Charlie Hebdo* and Paris attacks of 2015, allowing the police to carry out raids of businesses, houses of worship, and private residences without judicial review. Muslims can be placed under house arrest even if there is insufficient evidence to detain or charge them. These measures remain despite the fact that critics and even the Interior Ministry itself have pointed out the overall inefficacy of the new measures.[15]

All of these programs presume Muslims are guilty of terrorist tendencies simply because they are Muslim, not because of evidence of participation in criminal or terrorist activities. Put simply, Muslims are viewed not as citizens or residents with the same rights and privileges as majority populations but as suspects who must constantly prove their innocence under relentless scrutiny.

Detentions and Deportations

Shortly after the 9/11 attacks, the US Department of Justice (DOJ) detained approximately 1,200 Muslim and Arab men. The DOJ cited national security concerns for the detentions, but in the process, it refused to give many detainees access to legal representation, even as the US government attempted to uncover violations of the law and possible terrorism ties among those detained. This action led to complaints from civil liberties and human rights organization. A report from Human Rights Watch accused the government of presuming that the men in question were guilty simply because of their

Muslim backgrounds: "Being a male Muslim non-citizen from certain countries became a proxy for suspicious behavior."[16]

Many of these men, along with others who registered under NSEERS, faced deportation. More than 13,000 registrants with NSEERS underwent deportation proceedings.[17] In yet another DOJ deportation program, Operation Absconder, the US government attempted to deport 6,000 men, mostly from Middle Eastern countries, from a list of 314,000 individuals who were still present in the country even after receiving deportation orders. The majority of the 314,000 people came from Latin America, not the Middle East, so the focus on the 6,000 men from Middle Eastern countries was clearly targeting Muslims for deportation above other cultural or religious groups.[18]

Detentions and deportations of Muslim men constituted a key part of the US government's counterterrorism strategy in the first several years after 9/11. The United States received help from European police and security forces. In many instances, law enforcement agencies in Europe arrested and detained Muslim terrorism suspects and transferred them to US custody without judicial process.

Some suspects subsequently became victims of extraordinary rendition, a process whereby the United States transferred the suspects to countries or secret locations where they faced the possibility or reality of torture.[19] The CIA's rendition program relied on the assistance of European governments and made use of Europe's airports to transport suspects to secret interrogation and detention centers around the world. Some of these detention centers, also known as "black sites," were located in European countries such as Poland and Romania. The US Senate Intelligence Committee released a report in 2014 formally acknowledging detainees were tortured at these and other CIA black sites.[20]

A prominent example of extraordinary rendition involves the case of Abu Omar, an Egyptian national with Italian residency who was abducted from the streets of Milan by the CIA in 2003, allegedly with help from Italian officials. Abu Omar was thrown into a white van and rushed to a NATO airbase in northern Italy. From there, he was transferred onto a flight to another NATO airbase in Germany before being placed on a final flight to Cairo. In Cairo, he was detained by Egyptian officials for fourteen months. He was kept in a poorly ventilated, rat-infested cell and was tortured frequently. After his release, the case became public knowledge. A special prosecutor in Italy subsequently investigated what happened to Abu Omar. The investigation led to the conviction in absentia of over twenty CIA operatives.[21]

The extraordinary rendition and torture of Abu Omar, and many others like him, was illegal. The fact that such illegal acts endured for so long serves as a reminder that neither domestic nor international law is an obstacle when it comes to singling out Muslims for unjust if not brutal treatment in the name of national security.

The Electoral Politics of Islamophobia

The policies described so far reflect the erosion of basic civil liberties for Muslims in Western nations, under the assumption that Muslims are terrorist suspects because they are Muslim and not because they have disobeyed laws or incited violence. A quick glance at recent political rhetoric in Europe and the United States, often in conjunction with election cycles, suggests that prominent politicians are intensifying their efforts to target Muslim civil liberties and to tighten the presumed link between Islam and terrorism.

In Europe, we see this most clearly with far-right politicians whose political careers are dependent on anti-Muslim prejudice and racism. Marine Le Pen, leader of France's National Front and runner-up in the 2017 presidential elections, proposed banning headscarves from all public places and halal slaughtering of animals. She also advocated for dual French citizens to forfeit either their French or other foreign citizenship. This proposal targeted France's Muslim populations, many of whom have a North African background. Le Pen made it clear that French-Israeli dual citizenship, for example, would not be affected.[22]

In the Netherlands, Geert Wilders of the Party for Freedom has made a name for himself as Europe's most prominent anti-Muslim politician. Like Le Pen, Wilders was also the runner-up in the 2017 elections in his country. And like Le Pen, his platform promoted strong restrictions on Muslim civil liberties. In a one-page manifesto published on his website, Wilders promised that, if elected, his party would:

"de-Islamize the Netherlands" by barring immigrants from Muslim-majority countries, prohibiting headscarves at public functions, implementing "preventive detention of radical Muslims," closing all mosques and Islamic schools, and banning the Qur'an.[23]

The fact that Wilders and Le Pen could perform so well in their countries' respective elections with such hostile anti-Muslim proposals speaks volumes to the success they have had in linking all Muslims to terrorism. It also points to the uncertain future Muslim populations face in Europe when it comes to freedom of religion and civil liberties. In fact, restrictions on religious liberties for Muslims have been a reality for some time, particularly with the emergence of legislation in the past decade or more imposing bans in various countries on hijabs, full face veils, and minarets. Wilders and Le Pen are merely building on this anti-Muslim momentum.

In the United States, most election cycles in the post-9/11 era have witnessed spikes in anti-Muslim rhetoric. In 2007–2008, for example, rumors circulated that candidate Barack Obama was a Muslim, even though he is a Protestant Christian. A few volunteers for the Hillary Clinton campaign in Iowa helped spread this falsehood, as did operatives in the Republican Party. The rumor took hold and spread more broadly among the US population, prompting former Secretary of State Colin Powell to call out the prejudice driving the rumor in a television interview. "What if [Obama] is [a Muslim]? Is there something wrong with being a Muslim in this country? The answer is: No, that's not America."[24] But the rumor, and the anti-Muslim hostility driving it, didn't go away. Seven years later, a CNN poll found that three out of ten people still believed Obama was a Muslim, with 60 percent of Trump supporters holding this view.[25]

In the 2011 presidential GOP primaries, Herman Cain made headlines when he told a reporter that, if elected, he wouldn't consider appointing a Muslim as a federal judge or as a member of his cabinet. He argued that Muslim Americans should be barred from such positions because they are engaged in a "creeping attempt . . . to gradually ease Sharia law and the Muslim faith into our government."[26] Newt Gingrich, another presidential contender, compared Muslims to Nazis, insisting the former were trying to infiltrate the United States with an anti-American agenda just as the Nazis tried during World War II.[27]

But the 2015–2016 election cycle witnessed some of the worst anti-Muslim rhetoric and proposals to date from presidential candidates. Ben Carson, a retired neurosurgeon and early GOP frontrunner, fired the first shot. "I would not advocate that we put a Muslim in charge of this nation," Carson insisted during an interview on *Meet the Press*.[28] He justified this position by arguing that Islam is incompatible with the US Constitution, even though Article VI rules out imposing a religious test to qualify for public office in the United States.

In a follow-up interview, Carson doubled down on his position by employing arguments from anti-Muslim hate groups. He maintained that Sharia law conflicts with the

Constitution, an argument that draws on stereotypes of Sharia as focused on punishing adulterers and apostates as opposed to, say, the rituals required for prayer. Anti-Muslim individuals and organizations have used this argument to great success, as seen in the proposed legislation they have supported and fueled at the state level. Between 2010 and 2016, 194 anti-Sharia bills were proposed in 39 state legislatures. Eighteen of the bills have been enacted into law.[29] Carson knew what he was doing by raising the specter of Sharia.

Carson also asserted that Sharia requires Muslims to observe *taqiyya*, which he defined as a practice that "encourages you to lie to achieve your goals."[30] In other words, Sharia commands Muslims to deceive the rest of us, which means we can't trust Muslims. Ever. But what Carson said about *taqiyya* wasn't true. *Taqiyya* is a practice originating in Shiʻa Islam, though it has also been used by Sunni Muslims. It allows Muslims facing duress or persecution to withhold their true religious identity in order to spare themselves or others from suffering or death. It has nothing to do with encouraging Muslims to lie to non-Muslims in order to take over nations and impose some sort of totalitarian rule.

Ted Cruz, a senator from Texas who eventually finished second to Trump in the GOP primaries, raised eyebrows for a proposal he made after the Brussels terrorist attacks in March 2016. "We need to empower law enforcement to patrol and secure Muslim neighborhoods before they become radicalized," Cruz insisted. He believed Muslims were a threat simply because they were Muslims and that the only way to prevent them from engaging in terrorist activities was to impose some sort of police state on areas where they lived.

Critics pounced. Bill de Blasio, the mayor of New York City, stated that Cruz's comments had nothing to do with security and everything to do with demagoguery. Bill Bratton, the NYPD commissioner, noted that his department had close to one thousand Muslim officers. "Ironically," Bratton pointed out, "when [Cruz is] running around here, we probably have a few Muslim officers guarding him." Cruz remained undeterred. The origins of "radical Islamic terrorism" emanated from the Muslim community, he insisted, which means this community must be policed and scrutinized if this threat is to be eliminated.[31]

The GOP's eventual nominee unleashed a series of anti-Muslim proposals during his campaign, all predicated on the assumption that Muslims as a whole posed a clear and present danger to the nation. When pressed on national security in the aftermath of the November 2015 attacks in Paris, Trump indicated he would consider "drastic measures" when it came to monitoring Muslims, including ID cards and a comprehensive database.[32]

A few weeks later, Trump made his most outlandish proposal of the campaign. At a campaign rally in South Carolina, he read the following statement to an enthusiastic crowd: "Donald J. Trump is calling for a total and complete shutdown of Muslims entering the United States until our country's representatives can figure out what the hell is going on."[33] The proposal, which came just days after a terrorist attack in San Bernardino that killed fourteen people, was fervently embraced by many of Trump's core supporters. Just a few months later, majorities of Republican primary voters from Texas to Alabama to Virginia indicated their overwhelming support for the so-called "Muslim Ban" according to exit polling.[34]

Trump made other anti-Muslim statements and claims throughout the campaign, including the infamous "Islam hates us" remark. But it's the Muslim Ban that sticks out among all of his campaign proposals, not least of which because it was the one he pursued immediately after becoming president. In the first two months of his presidency, Trump issued two different executive orders aimed at curbing Muslim immigration and travel into the United States. The title of the two orders was revealing: "Protecting the Nation from Foreign Terrorist Entry into the United States."

Unlike the campaign promise, the orders did not target all Muslims but rather a handful of Muslim-majority countries. Even so, his earlier campaign rhetoric came back to haunt him as one court after another issued restraining orders on implementing the ban. The courts determined the intent behind the Muslim Ban was discriminatory and thereby a violation of the Establishment Clause in the First Amendment. This didn't cause the Trump administration to back down as it continued to fight for the ban. The priority that Trump gave the ban revealed just how important casting Muslims as the nation's greatest existential threat was to the White House. The ban helped Trump frame Muslims as hostile foreigners and "brown invaders," even though Muslims belong to a religious tradition that has existed in America since the earliest days of slavery.

All of these proposals came from Republican candidates and signaled a level of hostility that was a far cry not only from President Bush's insistence just after 9/11 that "Islam is peace," but from the openness the Republican Party once had for Muslims. We shouldn't forget that Muslims voted overwhelmingly for George W. Bush over his Democratic challenger Al Gore in 2000, with perhaps as many as 70 percent of Muslims choosing the GOP candidate.[35] But the Republican Party has increasingly alienated if not demonized Muslims in every election since then, largely due to the War on Terror and its ensuing counterterrorism policies. While this doesn't mean the Republican Party is inherently Islamophobic, it does suggest that the party has become more committed than ever to thinking of Muslims not as fellow citizens but as terrorist threats.

* * *

The politics and policies of linking Islam to terrorism are clear and consistent on both sides of the Atlantic. Muslims have become a securitized population—that is, Western governments have come to view Muslims primarily through the lens of national security. All of this presumes Muslims share some of the guilt for terrorist attacks carried out by extremists, for no other reason than they share a common religion. This presumption, as discussed in the previous chapter, doesn't stand up to the available evidence about what drives terrorism. Nor does it account for the many ways Muslims fight terrorism in word and deed, as we will see in the following section.

Notes

1. For the full text of the statement, see Just Action, "Statement on Islamophobia: Friendship Not Fear: Standing in Solidarity with Muslims at Luther College," Luther College, December 7, 2015, https://tinyurl.com/yccatcn5.

2. Jenna Johnson, "Trump Calls for 'Total and Complete Shutdown of Muslims Entering the United States,'" *Washington Post*, December 7, 2015, https://tinyurl.com/ybduwa34.

3. Samuel English, "Fighting Ignorance with Understanding," *Luther College Chips*, March 17, 2016, https://tinyurl.com/y8zmw9th.

4. Todd Green, "Professor Green Responds to Student on Civil Discourse," *Luther College Chips*, April 7, 2016, https://tinyurl.com/y7n27dul.

5. Office of the Secretary of the Department of Homeland Security, "Removing Designated Countries from the National Security Entry-Exit Registration System (NSEERS)," *Federal Register* 76, no. 82 (April 28, 2011): 23830–31, PDF, https://tinyurl.com/ycegatca.

6. "Information Sharing on Foreign Nationals: Border Security (Redacted)," Office of Inspector General, Department of Homeland Security, February 2012, PDF, https://tinyurl.com/yddyxjpw.

7. Arun Kundnani, *The Muslims Are Coming! Islamophobia, Extremism, and the Domestic War on Terror* (London: Verso, 2014), 156–57.

8. Todd H. Green, *The Fear of Islam: An Introduction to Islamophobia in the West* (Minneapolis: Fortress Press, 2015), 273–75.

9. Michael Barkun, "The FBI and American Muslims after September 11," in *The FBI and Religion: Faith and National Security Before and After 9/11*, ed. Sylvester A. Johnson and Steven Weitzman (Oakland: University of California Press, 2017), 247.

10. Barkun, "FBI and American Muslims," 271–73.

11. Human Rights Watch, "Illusion of Justice: Human Rights Abuses in US Terrorism Procedures," July 21, 2014, https://tinyurl.com/y7ezqck6.

12. Mark Townsend, "MI5 Pays UK Muslims to Spy on Terror Suspects," *The Guardian*, September 19, 2015, https://tinyurl.com/y874abs3; Green, *Fear of Islam*, 272.

13. Jahangir Mohammed and Adnan Siddiqui, "The Prevent Strategy: A Cradle to Grave Police-State," CAGE, 2013, https://tinyurl.com/ycbb2jrl.

14. Richard Adams, "Teachers Back Motion Calling for Prevent to Be Scrapped," *The Guardian*, March 28, 2016, https://tinyurl.com/ycccz4r.

15. Alissa J. Rubin, "Muslims in France Say Emergency Powers Go Too Far," *New York Times*, February 17, 2016, https://tinyurl.com/y97yhozr; Engy Abdelkader, "Are French Emergency Powers Becoming Permanent?," Berkley Center for Religion, Peace, and World Affairs, July 24, 2017, https://tinyurl.com/y9tfyl2q.

16. Cesar Munoz Acebes and Allyson Collins, "Presumption of Guilt: Human Rights Abuses of Post-September 11 Detainees," *Human Rights Watch* 14, no. 4 (2002): 4.

17. Rights Working Group, *The NSEERS Effect: A Decade of Racial Profiling, Fear, and Secrecy*, Penn State Law, May 2012, 9, PDF, https://tinyurl.com/y97mxsys.

18. John Tehranian, *Whitewashed: America's Invisible Middle Eastern Minority* (New York: New York University Press, 2009), 125.

19. Amnesty International, *State of Denial: Europe's Role in Rendition and Secret Detention* (London: Amnesty International, 2008), 1.

20. Senate Select Committee on Intelligence, *Committee Study of the Central Intelligence Agency's Detention and Interrogation Program: Findings and Conclusions*, December 3, 2014, http://tinyurl.com/hltk455.

21. Amnesty International, *State of Denial*, 55–58; Stephanie Kirchgaessner, "Former CIA Officer Faces Extradition to Italy over Abu Omar Kidnapping," *The Guardian*, April 25, 2016, https://tinyurl.com/ycdnlqpf.

22. Angelique Chrisafis, "'We Don't Want You Here': Muslims Fearful as France Prepares to Vote," *The Guardian*, May 5, 2017, https://tinyurl.com/yd7j97d3; Ethan B. Katz, "How Marine Le Pen

Relies on Dividing French Jews and Muslims," *The Atlantic*, April 19, 2017, https://tinyurl.com/y9u7d3tc.

23. Geert Wilders, "The Netherlands Ours Again!," *Geert Wilders Weblog*, August 26, 2016, https://tinyurl.com/yb2z9t9p.

24. Wajahat Ali, "Muslims for America," *The Guardian*, October 22, 2008, https://tinyurl.com/ya7bmsdc.

25. CNN/ORC International Poll, September 13, 2015, PDF, https://tinyurl.com/y96m8tk9.

26. Scott Keyes, "Herman Cain Tells ThinkProgress 'I Will Not' Appoint a Muslim in My Administration," ThinkProgress, March 26, 2011, https://tinyurl.com/ya66m6j2.

27. Huma Khan and Amy Bingham, "GOP Debate: Newt Gingrich's Comparison of Muslims and Nazis Sparks Outrage," ABC News, June 14, 2011, https://tinyurl.com/y7ayg8ja.

28. Ed Demaria, "Ben Carson Does Not Believe a Muslim Should Be President," NBC News, September 20, 2015, https://tinyurl.com/y8e9guce.

29. Elsadig Elsheikh, Basima Sisemore, and Natalia Ramirez Lee, *Legalizing Othering: The United States of Islamophobia*, Haas Institute for a Fair and Inclusive Society, University of California at Berkeley, September 2017, 7–8, PDF, https://tinyurl.com/yda59ag8.

30. Glenn Kessler, "Ben Carson's Claim That 'Taqiyya' Encourages Muslims 'to Lie to Achieve Your Goals,'" *Washington Post*, September 22, 2015, https://tinyurl.com/y8vo7zey.

31. Sam Sanders, "Ted Cruz Criticized after Suggesting Law Enforcement Patrol Muslim Areas," NPR, March 23, 2016, https://tinyurl.com/y89gbm8t.

32. Maggie Haberman and Richard Pérez-Peña, "Donald Trump Sets Off a Furor with Call to Register Muslims in the U.S.," *New York Times*, November 20, 2015, https://tinyurl.com/ycxs4wed.

33. Johnson, "Trump Calls for 'Total and Complete Shutdown.'"

34. Murtaza Hussain, "Huge Numbers of GOP Voters Favor Trump's Proposal to Ban Muslim Entry to U.S.," *The Intercept*, March 2, 2016, https://tinyurl.com/y8l4ot7a.

35. David A. Graham, "How Republicans Won and Then Lost the Muslim Vote," *The Atlantic*, December 9, 2015, https://tinyurl.com/y9cgbhux.

PART II

Ignoring Muslims Who Condemn Terrorism

3

Muslims Speak Out

A few weeks before Election Day in 2016, vandals fire-bombed the Republican headquarters in Orange County, North Carolina. On an adjacent building, the culprits spray-painted a swastika along with the words "Nazi Republicans leave town or else." When news of this story broke, one of my Facebook friends posted a message on my timeline. He asked me to condemn the attack. He assumed I had an obligation to do so since I spent so much time repudiating bigotry and hate crimes against Muslims. Certainly I should be willing to do the same when bigotry and violence are aimed at Republicans.

It was clear in the subsequent exchange that he believed my vocal opposition to the Islamophobia of the Trump campaign was part of the problem. He felt I was contributing to a hostile atmosphere that at least tacitly invited the kind of violence unleashed on the Republican office in North Carolina.

The reason this exchange sticks out to me is that it's the

only instance I can recall in which someone I know has singled me out and asked me to condemn hate-inspired violence committed by "my people." In every other instance when a hate crime, murder, or terrorist attack was committed by someone who looks like me or shares my cultural or religious background, I've always been given the benefit of the doubt. Always.

Take Dylann Roof, the white supremacist who killed nine African Americans during a Bible study in Charleston, South Carolina, in 2015. Roof and I share several things in common. He's white. So am I. His religious background is Lutheran. I teach at a Lutheran college and collaborate regularly with Lutheran organizations. He is a native Southerner. Me too. Despite these similarities, no one asked me to condemn Roof's murderous rampage. No one asked me to reject white supremacy or "Lutheran extremism." No one asked me, "Where are the moderate Southerners?" No one lumped me together with Roof. I was presumed innocent.

Muslims don't get the same benefit of the doubt. When someone with a Muslim background commits a terrorist attack, all Muslims are immediately and relentlessly put on the defensive with the usual questions. "Where are the moderate Muslims?" "Why don't Muslims speak out against terrorism?" Their experience is the opposite of my own.

Asking Muslims why they don't condemn terrorist attacks is unfair. It's also uninformed. We have plenty of evidence that Muslims overwhelmingly reject terrorism and violence that target civilians. A Gallup Poll conducted from 2001 to

2007 reveals that 93 percent of the world's Muslim population believes the 9/11 attacks were unjustified.[1] A 2017 poll from the Pew Research Center indicates that 76 percent of Muslim Americans believe targeting and killing civilians to further political, social, or religious goals is never justifiable, a higher percentage than white evangelical Protestants (59 percent), white mainline Protestants (59 percent), and Catholics (58 percent).[2]

Beyond the general attitudes of Muslims as measured by polls, we have the words of Muslim scholars, organizations, and activists. Muslims speak out against terrorism all the time. In fact, there are so many published statements, Facebook posts, and tweets made by Muslims against terrorism that it's impossible to keep track of them all, even with the help of websites devoted to this enormous task, such as Muslims Condemn.[3] And yet so few people seem to be aware of what Muslims are saying. That's the reason I'm devoting an entire chapter to this topic. It's time to bridge the gap between Muslim condemnations of terrorism and our unfamiliarity with these condemnations.

But how to proceed with such a discussion is tricky. After all, it would be mind-numbing to list all of the Muslim organizations and scholars that have made public statements condemning events such as 9/11, the Madrid and London bombings of 2004 and 2005, or the *Charlie Hebdo* and Paris attacks of 2015. The same goes for the many instances of Muslims condemning groups such as al-Qaeda or ISIS. Such lists might be informative, but they don't make for interesting (or memorable) reading.[4]

A better way forward is to focus on the reasons Muslims give for rejecting terrorism carried out in the name of Islam. Eight themes regularly surface in Muslim condemnations of terrorism. These themes reveal both how seriously Muslims take terrorism and how reliant they are on traditional Islamic sources and beliefs when condemning terrorism.

The Murder of Innocent People

One theme that is practically ubiquitous in Muslim condemnations of terrorism is the prohibition against murder. Islam strictly and unequivocally forbids the murder of innocent people. The verse from the Qur'an most often cited to justify this prohibition reads: "We decreed to the Children of Israel that if anyone kills a person . . . it is as if he kills all mankind" (Q. 5:32).[5] Yusuf al-Qaradawi, chair of the International Union of Muslim Scholars, views this verse as representative of Islam's teachings on the sanctity of human life. Islam, he argues, "holds the human soul in high esteem, and considers the attack against innocent human beings a grave sin."[6]

For many Muslim scholars, this verse applies no matter the political circumstances. Al-Qaradawi made this point explicitly after 9/11. He maintained that despite strong objections in the Muslim world to US foreign policy in the Middle East, including what he labeled as America's unfair policies on Israel, Islam is clear in its regard for the human soul. No act of violence against civilians can be justified, even if the political grievances behind the violence are legitimate.[7]

His views are shared by the Arab League, which insists that no matter what political differences exist between the United States and the Middle East, members of Arab and Muslim-majority nations share with America "the feelings of revulsion, horror and shock over the terrorist attack that ripped through the World Trade Centre and Pentagon."[8] Politics can't trump Islam's commitment to compassion and respect for innocent human life.

Many condemnations also spell out who is included among the innocent. For the Amman Message from 2004, a statement issued by the king of Jordan and later endorsed by hundreds of Muslim scholars, this list includes noncombatants, civilians, small children, school students, and the elderly.[9] Scholars such as Hamza Yusuf from the United States and Muhammad Tahir-ul-Qadri from Pakistan agree, adding that the Prophet Muhammad also forbade the killing of women and religious professionals, including rabbis, priests, and nuns.[10]

Muslim scholars do not deny that Islam allows for the killing of other human beings under specified circumstances, particularly in defensive situations. But Muslims who transgress the limits imposed by God and take the lives of innocent people are no martyrs. They are murderers.

The Killing of Emissaries

If there was one event that made politicians and the larger public wake up to the dangers posed by ISIS, it was the successive beheadings of two American journalists captured on video. James Foley was beheaded in August 2014 after being abducted almost two years earlier in Syria. Steven Sotloff was beheaded the following month, also after being abducted and held captive in Syria.

These brutal killings prompted Muslims scholars to make specific statements on what Islam requires concerning the treatment of emissaries and other people who enter Muslim lands as guests. The clearest statement comes from the *Letter to Baghdadi*, a detailed condemnation of ISIS and its leader, Abu Bakr al-Baghdadi, originally issued and signed by over one hundred Muslim scholars not long after Sotloff's beheading. The letter draws on the *Sunna*, the example established by the words and deeds of the Prophet Muhammad, in insisting that Islam forbids the killing of emissaries because the Prophet himself forbade it. The letter defines emissaries not only as official diplomats but as anyone who is sent from one community to another "to perform a noble task such as reconciliation or the delivery of a message." This includes journalists, whom the letter describes as "emissaries of truth, because their job is to expose the truth to people in general."[11]

The Syrian scholar Shaykh Muhammad al-Yaqoubi explains the Islamic rationale for protecting the lives of emissaries in contractual terms. According to a story from the hadith, the authoritative collection of Muhammad's words and deeds, the Prophet said: "Whoever kills a non-Muslim under contract will never smell the scent of paradise." The Prophet also stated: "When a Muslim offers protection to a non-Muslim, it is a covenant and it goes for all. Anyone who breaches this covenant shall have upon him a curse from Allah, the angels, and all mankind."[12] Al-Yaqoubi considers any harm done to those entering Muslim lands in the spirit of peace an egregious violation of this covenant and at odds with Islamic tradition. Al-Yaqoubi adds that it's not only journalists and diplomats who are to be protected by this covenant but also foreign residents, tourists, students, and aid workers.[13]

The Proper Understanding of Jihad

After the 9/11 attacks, *jihad* entered the everyday vocabulary of Americans and Europeans. Jihad literally means "struggle" and refers variously to actions in defense of Islam, the fight against sinful inclinations, or the quest for social justice. Yet the word has become shorthand for "holy war" and even "terrorism" in the ears of many. It's almost impossible to hear the word today without conjuring up images of angry ISIS soldiers or suicide bombers yelling "Allahu Akbar" before blowing up or massacring innocent people. Muslim scholars, however, believe violent extremists have hijacked the concept of jihad and have made it almost impossible for ordinary Muslims to appeal to the language of jihad to articulate a positive vision of their faith.

What is clear in Muslim condemnations of groups such as al-Qaeda and ISIS is that jihad has nothing to do with terrorism. Jihad does not pertain to the indiscriminate killing of innocent people in the name of God, nor does it allow for self-sacrifice in the form of suicide bombings or the hijacking and crashing of airplanes. Syed Shahabuddin, the late Indian Muslim politician, put it bluntly: "Islam prohibits terrorism as well as suicide. Jihad is neither and has no place for taking innocent lives or one's own life."[14]

Jihad does allow for defensive force to be used when the Muslim community comes under attack. The *Letter to Baghdadi* invokes the Qur'an to support this interpretation: "Fight in God's cause against those who fight you, but do not overstep the limits. God does not love those who overstep the limits" (Q. 2:190). This verse indicates that while Muslims can defend themselves from attack, God has imposed limits on war. According to traditional Islamic law, the rules of warfare include securing the lives and property of noncombatants; doing no harm to women, children, the elderly, and invalids; protecting houses of worship; and refraining from torturing prisoners. These legal provisions reflect an understanding of defensive war that is quite close to some Christian views about ethical warfare.

Scholars also are quick to invoke a distinction made by the Prophet Muhammad between the lesser and greater jihad. The *Letter to Baghdadi* argues that according to the Prophet, the lesser jihad pertains to struggling and fighting against one's enemies. But the greater jihad takes precedence. The greater jihad is a struggle against selfishness. It involves "remembrance of God and purification of the soul."[15] Abdulaziz Sachedina, an American Muslim scholar, agrees that the greater jihad facing Muslims is the "struggle with one's ego and false pride."[16]

For the overwhelming majority of Muslims, the day-to-day jihad they wage does not rely on bombs and bullets. Jihad is the spiritual quest to become a better human being by avoiding egotism, being honest, and performing good deeds. This "struggle of the soul," moreover, is not an innovation in the meaning of the word. As Asma Afsaruddin of Indiana University notes, this internal, spiritual struggle has featured prominently among Muslim scholars throughout Islamic history.[17]

Jihad is also the endeavor to make the world a more just, more humane place. Linda Sarsour, a prominent Muslim American activist, illustrates this by citing a hadith concerning a man who asked the Prophet about the best form of jihad. The Prophet responded: "A word of truth in front of a tyrant ruler or leader." Sarsour adds that speaking truth to power is essential in the nonviolent quest for justice, whether that quest is taking place in the Middle East or in the United States.[18]

The Use of Torture

There's no shortage of stories circulating in the media about ISIS torturing prisoners and enemies. The most high-profile instances are videotaped and released on the Internet, such as the burning alive of a Jordanian fighter pilot in 2015 or of two Turkish soldiers in 2016. But we know from those who have survived ISIS prisons that torture is a widespread tactic, irrespective of whether the cameras are rolling. ISIS soldiers have been known to rape women (and to attempt to sanctify the act by praying in front of the victim before and after), to beat and starve prisoners, to waterboard captives, to threaten prisoners with death, to decapitate victims with knives, and to bury defectors alive.

Their actions have prompted strong condemnations from Muslim scholars. Arguments employed against ISIS-inspired torture focus on the actions of the Prophet Muhammad and other prominent figures of the Islamic tradition. Drawing on one of the hadith, Al-Yaqoubi argues the Prophet Muhammad strictly forbade torture by fire. In fact, the Prophet forbade torture altogether, teaching that if a Muslim must take the life of another for a just reason, this must be done in an ethical, merciful manner. ISIS, Al-Yaqoubi points out, violates the principles of Islam by torturing and mutilating people to death.[19]

In "A New Muslim Statement against Torture" (2009), prominent Muslim American journalists and activists note the Islamic tradition abounds with stories demanding Muslims condemn torture, irrespective of who the perpetrators are. These stories include the Prophet Moses (Musa), who gave up his royal position to stop torture; the Prophet Jesus (Isa), who was a victim of torture by an unjust government; and the

Prophet Muhammad's grandson Hussain, whose camp once was deprived of food and water.[20]

Muslim scholars advocating for the humane and merciful treatment of prisoners often appeal to the Prophet's actions at the Battle of Badr in 624. According to Islamic tradition, the Prophet ordered: "Take heed of the recommendation to treat the prisoners fairly." The Prophet also demanded clothes be provided to one prisoner who had none.[21] Shaykh Abdool Rahman Khan, representing the Council for Social Justice for the Islamic Circle of North America, argues Muhammad's mercy extended to the needs of all prisoners at this battle. The Prophet saw to it that food and water were given to all, and he assured freedom for any prisoner who could teach Muslims to read. The example of the Prophet, insists Khan, gives no allowance for inflicting pain and suffering on other human beings.[22]

It's also worth pointing out the National Religious Campaign against Torture (NRCAT) has a number of Islamic organizations on its membership roster. While NRCAT is dedicated primarily to eradicating US-sponsored torture, it appeals broadly to religious values of human dignity in its opposition to torture no matter who is perpetrating it. The Islamic organizations that have formally endorsed NRCAT's mission include the Islamic Society of North America, the Islamic Circle of North America, the Council on American-Islamic Relations, and the Muslim Public Affairs Council.

The False Practice of *Takfir*

In light of ISIS's high-profile attacks in Western cities, including Paris and Brussels, it's tempting to conclude non-Muslim Europeans and Americans are the primary victims of the terrorist organization. Not so. The overwhelming majority of ISIS's victims are Muslims. The reason this is significant is that Islam has a long tradition of prohibiting violence and bloodshed between Muslims outside the context of war. As the *Letter to Baghdadi* states: "It is not permissible to kill any Muslim, (nor indeed any human being), who is unarmed and a non-combatant."[23] Such actions are strictly prohibited in the Qur'an: "If anyone kills a believer deliberately, the punishment for him is Hell, and there he will remain: God is angry with him, and rejects him, and has prepared a tremendous torment for him" (Q. 4:93).

ISIS circumvents such prohibitions by engaging in *takfir*. *Takfir* refers to the practice of declaring another Muslim an apostate. It's roughly akin to excommunication in Christianity. ISIS employs *takfir* as one of its key strategies. It paints all Muslims who reject its version of Islam as apostates. ISIS then justifies the shedding of Muslim blood in terrorist attacks by insisting the victims aren't true Muslims.

The *Letter to Baghdadi* reminds ISIS's leadership that anyone who recites the *Shahada*, or the confession of faith, is a Muslim: "There is no god but God, and Muhammad is the Messenger of God." The Qur'an forbids labeling any Muslim a non-Muslim without due cause: "So, you who believe, be careful when you go to fight in God's way, and do not say to someone who offers you a greeting of peace, 'You are not a believer,' out of desire for the chance gains of this life—God has plenty of gains for you. You yourself were in the same position [once], but God was gracious to you, so be careful: God is fully aware of what you do" (Q. 4:94).

The letter also appeals to a story that occasioned this particular verse. When Osama bin Zayd, the son of one of Muhammad's adopted sons, killed a Muslim who had recited the *Shahada*, the Prophet asked why. Osama defended his actions by claiming the man was not sincere in his confession of faith since he was only trying to spare his own life. The Prophet responded: "Did you see inside his heart to know whether or not he meant it?"[24] The point of the hadith is to warn against claiming the authority to judge who is and isn't a real Muslim. That judgement is left to God.

The Reinstitution of Slavery

The majority of Muslim nations abolished and criminalized slavery over a century ago. In recent years, this consensus against slavery has been challenged by the likes of Boko Haram and ISIS, both of which have reinstituted slavery by enslaving girls and women. Abubakar Shekau, the leader of Boko Haram, insists Islam justifies the practice: "Slavery is allowed in my religion, and I shall capture people and make them slaves."[25] An article from *Dabiq*, ISIS's English-language magazine, argues that "enslaving the families of (non-believers) and taking their women as concubines is a firmly established aspect of Shariah."[26] ISIS believes Yazidis—a Kurdish-speaking community whose religion contains elements of Zoroastrianism, Christianity, and Islam —are idolaters and thus fair game when it comes to slavery.

The *Letter to Baghdadi* refutes ISIS's reinstitution of slavery in detail. The letter takes issue with appeals to the Sharia to justify slavery: "You have resuscitated something that the Shari'ah has worked tirelessly to undo and has been considered forbidden by consensus for over a century."[27] Muslim countries throughout the world, the letter points out, have signed antislavery conventions. On this point, Al-Yaqoubi notes Muslims are bound by God to remain faithful to the covenants and contracts they enter into concerning the prohibition of slavery.[28]

The Qur'an serves as the basis for prohibiting slavery according to the *Letter to Baghdadi*. "What will explain to you what the steep path is? It is to free a slave" (Q. 90:12–13). The letter also appeals to the example of the Prophet who "freed all male and female slaves who were in his possession or who had been given to him."[29]

None of this means Islam is beyond reproach when it comes to its history with slavery. One can even question whether the *Letter to Baghdadi* is correct when it argues that "one of Islam's aims is to abolish slavery."[30] At the very least, this claim is ahistorical.[31] Slavery was pervasive in the world in which Islam arose. The Qur'an, like the Jewish and Christian scriptures, assumes the practice. And as mentioned above, according to Islamic tradition, the Prophet himself had slaves (though he also freed them).[32] But the larger point made by the letter stands when viewed from a contemporary perspective. The overwhelming majority of Muslim scholars believe the trajectory within Islamic sources and traditions moves toward the repudiation of slavery, not the reinstitution of it.

The Practice of Forced Conversions

In August 2014, ISIS fighters surrounded the small village of Kocho in northern Iraq. They gave the Yazidi villagers a choice—convert or die. When the ISIS-imposed deadline for conversion expired just over a week later, the fighters stormed the village, killed the men, and abducted the women and children.

The episode illustrates one of ISIS's strategies toward Yazidis and other communities: forced conversion. This practice reinforces stereotypes many in the West have of Islam as a religion of the sword and coercion. But forced conversion is a practice roundly condemned by Muslim scholars and organizations. The Muslim Public Affairs Council states it most bluntly in its "Declaration against Extremism": "In Islam, true faith is incompatible with coercion."[33] Muhammad Tahir-ul-Qadri elaborates on this principle by insisting that Islam "requires the confirmation and conviction of the heart."[34] The heart, Qadri insists, cannot be coerced.

Muslims often cite the Qur'an in defense of religious freedom, particularly: "There is no compulsion in religion" (Q. 2:256). Some scholars in Islamic history have argued this verse was abrogated. Abrogation (*naskh*) is a controversial doctrine that refers to a later revelation superseding an earlier revelation. Those who believe 2:256 was abrogated argue it was an early revelation to Muhammad, but that God revealed other verses later in Muhammad's career, particularly verses pertaining to warfare, that nullified this verse.

Most scholars reject the notion that this verse was abrogated. The *Letter to Baghdadi* argues the verse was revealed to Muhammad after the conquest of Mecca and thus is of a later date. The editors of *The Study Qur'an* also point out abrogation is a practice that refers to legal commands and not to descriptions of history, ethics, or God's nature.[35] It's impossible for 2:256 to be abrogated since it is not a legal command. ISIS's practice of forced conversion therefore runs counter to the Qur'an and the overwhelming consensus of present-day Muslim scholars.

The Treatment of People of the Book

Yazidis are not the only people targeted by ISIS for forced conversions and executions. Christians are as well. In fact, ISIS has treated practically all religious minorities as enemies and combatants, torturing them, enslaving them, deporting them, murdering them, and destroying their homes and houses of worship. This treatment runs contrary to the special esteem Islam provides "People of the Book" (*Ahl al-Kitab*), a category that refers to Jews, Christians, and other communities to whom God previously revealed scriptures via particular messengers. Some Muslim scholars include Yazidis as People of the Book.[36]

The basis for treating People of the Book with respect and dignity is the Qur'an. *A Common Word between Us and You* (2007),[37] an open letter written by Muslim leaders to their Christian counterparts to set forth common ground between the two religions, references this key verse: "Say, 'People of the Book,' let us arrive at a statement that is common to us all: we worship God alone, we ascribe no partner to Him, and none of us takes others beside God as lords" (Q. 3:64). Jews and Christians, in other words, possess a common vocabulary with Muslims, and all worship "God alone."

Muslim scholars also argue that treatment of People of the Book is modeled on the Prophet Muhammad and the earliest generations of Muslims. The *Letter to Baghdadi* insists religious minorities such as Christians "are friends, neighbors and cocitizens." Their ancestors fought alongside Muhammad's army against the Byzantines and therefore have been citizens in Muslim lands since that time. Indeed, covenants and agreements have been established between Christians and other Islamic empires in history. This means "they are not strangers to these lands but friends."[38]

Based on the treatment accorded to People of the Book by Muhammad, along with the agreements and declarations upheld by Muslims toward religious minorities in the earliest generations of Islam, Muhammad Tahir-ul-Qadri argues non-Muslims possess the following rights in Muslim-majority nations:[39]

1. Equal treatment under the law
2. Protection of their religion from harm

3. Protection of life, property, and honor
4. Appointment to high administrative positions
5. Freedom to appoint their own religious leaders and officeholders
6. Protection of their houses of worship

ISIS has violated all of these rights according to Qadri and many other Muslim scholars.

Aside from obvious examples of physical harm and forced conversions already mentioned, ISIS has targeted and destroyed churches and many other houses of worship. Shaykh Muhammad al-Yaqoubi condemns these actions based on this verse:[40] "If God did not repel some people by means of others, many monasteries, churches, synagogues, and mosques, where God's name is invoked, would have been destroyed" (Q. 22:40). According to Qadri, the Prophet Muhammad observed reverence for houses of worship and protected them from destruction even after hard-fought battles against people of other faiths. Such was the case after the Battle of Khaybar in 628 when the Prophet prevented the houses of worship from being destroyed.[41] The Qur'an and examples of the Prophet make it clear Muslims must use force to defend the houses of worship that utter God's name.

ISIS's oppression of People of the Book has resulted in growing pressure on Muslim scholars to speak out on behalf of religious minorities in Muslim-majority lands. One response to this pressure is the Marrakesh Declaration, a statement issued by over 250 Muslim scholars in early 2016 in defense of freedom of religion for religious minorities. The

Declaration calls upon politicians, lawmakers, educators, and many others "to establish a broad movement for the just treatment of religious minorities in Muslim countries" and to create awareness for the rights these minorities possess. The Declaration makes it clear that denial of freedom of religion runs contrary to the practice of the Prophet Muhammad as enshrined in the Charter of Medina, a document written by the Prophet in 622 that granting religious freedom to people of other faiths in Medina.[42]

* * *

All of this content is easy to find. You don't need access to a university library or to have proficiency in Arabic or other foreign languages to find this information. Much of it is in English and literally available at your fingertips.

When someone asks me, "Why don't Muslims condemn terrorism?," I sometimes respond: "Have you ever Googled, 'Muslims condemning terrorism?'" It's hard not to say this without sounding like a smart-ass. But it's a legitimate question. We use Google for pretty much everything else. The directions to a local dog park. A recipe for rhubarb pie. The kickoff time for the Super Bowl. The weather forecast for tomorrow's rush hour commute. So why don't many of us think to Google, "Muslims condemning terrorism"? Within seconds, we would have access to internet sites introducing us to these condemnations. If we change the Google search to "Muslims protesting terrorism," we would find stories of ordinary Muslims taking to the streets to demonstrate against terrorism from Barcelona to Paris to Mumbai. And yet I encounter many people who have never done a simple Google search on either of these topics.

The most important question we should be asking ourselves is why many of us don't know about these condemnations, particularly in light of how easy it is to find this information. It's clearly not because the majority population is unintelligent or willfully ignorant. It's because too many politicians and journalists have perpetuated the narrative that Muslims are silent on terrorism. They are the ones who keep asking the question, "Why don't Muslims condemn terrorism?" as if Muslims never do. We've been taught, even encouraged, to believe it's just common sense that Muslims aren't speaking out against al-Qaeda, Boko Haram, or ISIS. Because many public figures link Islam to violence in explicit and implicit ways, many of us don't question the question.

Our ignorance about what Muslims are saying about terrorism is understandable given the sources of our "knowledge" of Muslim communities. But those of us in the majority population can no longer afford to be naïve. We have a moral responsibility to correct this story. It falls on us to do our homework and learn what Muslims are saying against terrorism. It falls on us to call out politicians and journalists who ask uninformed questions of our Muslim neighbors and who do so without doing their own homework—or Google searches for that matter. It falls on us to tell the truth about our Muslim neighbors and their many condemnations of terrorism.

Notes

1. John L. Esposito and Dalia Mogahed, *Who Speaks for Islam? What a Billion Muslims Really Think* (New York: Gallup, 2007), 69–70.

2. "Terrorism and Concerns about Extremism," Pew Research Center, July 26, 2017, https://tinyurl.com/y7hjzgh9.

3. See https://muslimscondemn.com/.

4. For additional websites that contain sample lists of Muslim scholars and organizations that have spoken out against terrorism since 9/11, see Charles Kurzman, "Islamic Statements against Terrorism," University of North Carolina, September 17, 2001, https://tinyurl.com/y9r9re4d; and Todd Green, "Muslims Condemning Terrorism," The Fear of Islam, https://tinyurl.com/y8mvuuwe.

5. For the sake of consistency, all citations from the Qur'an, unless otherwise stated, come from M. A. S. Abdel Haleem, *The Qur'an* (New York: Oxford University Press, 2005). This includes Qur'anic citations from authors and texts that originally relied on other English translations.

6. Tamara Sonn, *Is Islam an Enemy of the West?* (Malden, MA: Polity, 2016), 47.

7. "Sheikh Yusuf al-Qaradawi Condemns Attacks against Civilians: Forbidden in Islam," *IslamOnline*, September 13, 2001, https://tinyurl.com/ya3dm9vf.

8. Kurzman, "Islamic Statements against Terrorism."

9. The Amman Message, November 2004, https://tinyurl.com/y76q34z7.

10. Richard Scheinin, "Expert Says Islam Prohibits Violence against Innocents," *The Mercury News*, September 15, 2001, https://tinyurl.com/yamwlmsx; Muhammad Tahir-ul-Qadri, *Fatwa on Terrorism and Suicide Bombings* (London: Minhaj-ul-Quran International, 2010), 131–32.

11. *Open Letter to Dr. Ibrahim Awwad al-Badri, Alias 'Abu Bakr al-Baghdadi,' and to the Fighters and Followers of the Self-Declared 'Islamic State,'* September 19, 2004, 9, PDF, www.lettertobaghdadi.com.

12. Shaykh Muhammad al-Yaqoubi, *Refuting ISIS: Destroying Its Religious Foundations and Proving It Has Strayed from Islam and That*

Fighting It Is an Obligation (Herndon, VA: Sacred Knowledge, 2016), 33.

13. Al-Yaqoubi, *Refuting ISIS*, 33.

14. Syed Shahabuddin, "Global War against Terrorism—The Islamic Dimension," *The Mill Gazette*, November 1, 2001, https://tinyurl.com/yd4mgdel.

15. *Open Letter to Baghdadi*, 6.

16. Abdulaziz Sachedina, "Where Was God on September 11?," Islam and Islamic Studies Resources, University of Georgia, https://tinyurl.com/yde4k9wb.

17. Asma Afsaruddin, "How I Explained to My Impressionable Student That Islam Is Not Monolithic," *Huffington Post*, January 12, 2016, https://tinyurl.com/y8clnnuz.

18. Abigail Abrams, "Women's March Organizer Linda Sarsour Spoke of 'Jihad.' But She Wasn't Talking about Violence," *Time*, July 7, 2017, https://tinyurl.com/y8dy377w.

19. Al-Yaqoubi, *Refuting ISIS*, 11–12.

20. Hussein Rashid, "A New Muslim Statement against Torture," *Religion Dispatches*, May 8, 2009, https://tinyurl.com/yb95kkbr.

21. C. G. Weeramantry, *Islamic Jurisprudence: An International Perspective* (New York: St. Martin's, 1988), 135.

22. Shaykh Abdool Rahman Khan, "Islam Condemns Torture," ICNA Council for Social Justice, May 13, 2014, https://tinyurl.com/y7drhbza.

23. *Open Letter to Baghdadi*, 9.

24. *Open Letter to Baghdadi*, 9.

25. Tim Lister, "Boko Haram: The Essence of Terror," CNN, October 22, 2014, https://tinyurl.com/yc4kbnna.

26. "Islamic State Seeks to Justify Enslaving Yazidi Women and Girls in Iraq," *Newsweek*, October 13, 2014, https://tinyurl.com/ycr4vzhq.

27. *Open Letter to Baghdadi*, 12.

28. Al-Yaqoubi, *Refuting ISIS*, 15–16.

29. *Open Letter to Baghdadi*, 12.

30. *Open Letter to Baghdadi*, 12.

31. Kecia Ali, "Redeeming Slavery: The 'Islamic State' and the Quest

for Islamic Morality," *Mizan* 1, no. 1 (2016): 6, PDF, https://tinyurl.com/y7aozog4.

32. Kecia Ali, "The Truth about Islam and Sex Slavery History Is More Complicated Than You Think," *Huffington Post*, August 19, 2016, http://tinyurl.com/ybthg4j7.

33. Muslim Public Affairs Council, "Declaration against Extremism," PDF, https://tinyurl.com/y8zuzjjn.

34. Qadri, *Fatwa on Terrorism*, 160.

35. Seyyed Hossein Nasr, ed., *The Study Quran: A New Translation and Commentary* (New York: HarperOne, 2015), 49, 112.

36. See *Open Letter to Baghdadi*, 11–12.

37. *A Common Word between Us and You*, MABDA 20 (Amman: Royal Aal Al-Bayt Institute for Islamic Thought, 2012), PDF available at ACommonWord.com.

38. *Open Letter to Baghdadi*, 11.

39. Qadri, *Fatwa on Terrorism*, 145.

40. Al-Yaqoubi, *Refuting ISIS*, 14.

41. Al-Yaqoubi, *Refuting ISIS*, 162–63.

42. "Executive Summary of the Marrakesh Declaration on the Rights of Religious Minorities in Predominantly Muslim Majority Countries," Marrakesh Declaration, January 25–27, 2016, PDF, https://tinyurl.com/yaf7s2nz.

4

Muslims Take Action

In my time as a State Department advisor, I interacted with plenty of people who were in the business of countering terrorism and violent extremism. Some of these folks were Muslims or had a Muslim background. Like everyone else, they worked long hours and endured lots of stress to, in the words of the mission statement, "create a more secure, democratic, and prosperous world for the benefit of the American people and the international community."[1] Their names aren't known to the larger public, and that's no accident. A certain degree of anonymity comes with the territory of working at the State Department. If rank-and-file employees do their jobs well, you will never hear about them in the news.

The Muslims I had the privilege of knowing at State didn't seek the limelight, but the limelight sometimes sought them. We can thank the professional Islamophobia network for that. This network consists of far-right politicians, activists, bloggers, pseudo-scholars, and authors who make a living and a career off of demonizing Muslims and casting Islam in the worst possible light. According to one study of thirty-three anti-Muslim organizations in the United States, this network had a combined revenue of $205 million dollars between 2008–2013.[2] Leaders of these organizations have increasingly gained access to powerful media and political platforms to amplify their messages of fear and hatred. We're talking about people such as Robert Spencer, director of Jihad Watch; Pamela Geller, blogger and cofounder (along with Spencer) of the American Freedom Defense Initiative; Frank Gaffney, president of the Center for Security Policy; and Brigitte Gabriel, the head of ACT for America.

This powerful network has insisted for years that the Muslim Brotherhood—a political movement that calls for the establishment of Islamic principles in government—has infiltrated the State Department and other federal agencies. In 2012, the reach of this far-fetched conspiracy theory extended all the way into Congress as a handful of far-right representatives, led by Michele Bachmann, wrote a letter to the inspector general of the State Department falsely accusing Huma Abedin, the deputy chief of staff of Secretary of State Hillary Clinton, of having ties to the Muslim Brotherhood. The accusations were absurd, but in an age of rampant Islamophobia, it doesn't take much for the most ridiculous claims about Muslims to get treated as alternative facts.

Suspicions that Muslim Brotherhood sympathizers are embedded in the State Department and other federal agencies have persisted. President Trump, his closest advisors, and prominent members of Congress have trafficked in these kinds of anti-Muslim conspiracy theories. Steve Bannon, the former White House chief strategist, has repeatedly insisted radical Muslims with terrorist agendas have penetrated the highest levels of government.[3] He has a kindred spirit in Congress in Ted Cruz. Cruz, who relies heavily on the counsel of anti-Muslim conspiracy theorist Frank Gaffney, has spent years trying to have the Muslim Brotherhood labeled a "foreign terrorist organization" by the US government.

For their part, Muslims employed by the federal government continue to serve with distinction despite accusations their true loyalties lie with an organization that presumably is trying to destroy the country from within. I have a high regard for my Muslim friends at State who are committed to working for a more secure, prosperous world despite the fact that they are sometimes held in contempt by the government they serve. The same holds true for Muslim politicians in Congress, such as Keith Ellison and André Carson, and for Muslims serving in many other branches of government.

In his "Letter from a Birmingham Jail" (1963), Martin Luther King Jr. reflects on examples of courage in the Civil Rights movement, from bus boycotts to lunch-counter sit-ins. It's in this context that he remarks: "One day the South will recognize its real heroes."[4] The real heroes won't be people who preach hatred against the oppressed or who unjustly use violence in the name of law and order. These heroes will be women and men dedicated to dismantling a system that relies on violence to undermine the rights and dignity of all people.

I've been thinking about King's reflections quite a bit while writing this book. It has become my hope that one of these days, we will recognize our real heroes in the fight against terrorism. These heroes will not be xenophobic politicians who galvanize voters by insinuating that Muslims, immigrants, and refugees represent the ultimate threat to national security. Nor will they be hate groups that peddle conspiracy theories about a Muslim "fifth column" infiltrating Western governments.

Our real heroes will be the Muslim women and men who were willing to take action against the threat of terrorism, in some instances putting their lives on the line, even as they faced suspicion and at times outright hatred from some of their non-Muslim neighbors. These heroes will also include Muslims whose names we may never know, either because their work required anonymity or because their deeds were performed outside the gaze of the media.

Muslim Nations Fighting Terrorism

Although this chapter focuses on Muslims living in Western nations, it's worth beginning our discussion with Muslim-majority countries that have helped the West in its fight against terrorism. Complaints that Muslims aren't doing anything to combat terrorism, or aren't doing enough, miss the most obvious point. The US-led invasions of Afghanistan and

Iraq, which served as the backbone for the War on Terror, were made possible with help from Muslim allies abroad.

The initial military response to the 9/11 attacks was Operation Enduring Freedom. It began with US and British airstrikes on al-Qaeda and Taliban targets in Afghanistan in October 2001. Many countries lent assistance to this campaign, including Muslim-majority nations. Some of this assistance was substantial. Turkey sent personnel to both US Central Command and European Command to help with efforts in the war in Afghanistan. Turkey also sent troops to Afghanistan to train Afghan allies and deployed ships that monitored and intercepted vessels believed to be supporting al-Qaeda and the Taliban. Pakistan provided logistical support for US troops in Afghanistan, a necessity since Afghanistan is landlocked. Much of the supplies and equipment to US troops were shipped into Karachi before being delivered into Afghanistan.

A much smaller country, Albania, also contributed to the cause, offering intelligence, diplomatic, and military support to the operation and allowing coalition forces to use its airspace, bases, and ports. Many other Muslim-majority countries, from Bahrain to Bangladesh offered coalition forces the use of military bases, airspace, and seaports. The International Security Assistance Force, a NATO-sponsored security mission in Afghanistan, was led by Turkey and included countries such as Albania, Bahrain, Jordan, and the United Arab Emirates (UAE).[5]

Operation Iraqi Freedom proved far more controversial

among Muslim-majority countries. The United States struggled to secure the same degree of support it had grown accustomed to in Afghanistan. This was mostly due to the unpersuasive arguments from the US government that an invasion of Iraq was a necessary response to the 9/11 attacks and that the Saddam Hussein regime possessed weapons of mass destruction. Some of the strong alliances from Operation Enduring Freedom quickly broke down when it came to Iraq.

Turkey, a major partner in the war in Afghanistan, was less eager to help out in the Iraq War. The Turkish parliament rejected a government motion to allow for the deployment of 62,000 US troops, 255 jet aircraft, and 65 helicopters in Turkey.[6] Saudi Arabia, whose Prince Sultan Air Base played a significant role in air operations in Afghanistan, expressed such opposition to the Iraq War that the United States moved significant weapons, equipment, and troops from that base to Al Udeid Air Base in Qatar for the invasion of Iraq.

In fact, when it comes to Arab nations, the majority opposed the Iraq War. Kuwait was the only member of the Arab League to openly support it. But that doesn't mean other Muslim-majority nations failed to offer assistance. Most of them helped but did so without drawing much public attention to their efforts or by restricting the degree of assistance. Saudi Arabia did allow overflights of US missiles and aircraft, as did Jordan. Egypt allowed the US military free passage through the Suez Canal, along with granting access to airspace. Turkey allowed humanitarian flights and the airlifting of the wounded among coalition forces. Smaller countries such as Albania, Azerbaijan, and Bosnia and Herzegovina contributed troops to the coalition.

Since 2014, the fight against terrorism in the Middle East has been focused on the spread of ISIS in Syria and Iraq. Muslim-majority countries that have offered either military or nonmilitary assistance to this effort include Turkey, Kuwait, the United Arab Emirates, Egypt, Jordan, Malaysia, and Albania. Just as important are the Muslim soldiers in Iraq and Syria who are literally on the front lines in the fight against ISIS. When we hear stories of Iraqi forces retaking cities such as Fallujah and Mosul from ISIS, we should remember that the religious makeup of these forces is overwhelmingly Muslim.

When pundits insist Muslims abroad aren't doing much to combat terrorism, it's important to point to this evidence and make clear that military responses to the Taliban, al-Qaeda, and ISIS have always involved Muslims and Muslim-majority countries.

Muslims Serving in the Armed Forces

In June 2004, Captain Humayun Khan of the US Army Reserves died in Iraq while serving his country. Born in the United Arab Emirates into a family with Pakistani roots, Khan grew up in the Washington, DC, area, graduated from the University of Virginia in 2000, and was commissioned in the Army shortly thereafter. In 2004, he was deployed to Iraq for Operation Iraqi Freedom. Four months into his tour,

Khan was inspecting soldiers near a guard post. As a vehicle approached his compound at a fast speed, he ordered his soldiers to stay put while he moved forward to signal to the driver. An improvised explosive device inside the car detonated, killing Khan, two Iraqi civilians, and two insurgents.

Khan was awarded the Bronze Star and Purple Heart for his actions. He was buried in Arlington National Cemetery and received full military honors, as would be expected. Khan's burial was also accompanied by Islamic funeral prayers, while his headstone was inscribed not with a cross but a crescent, the symbol of Islam. Khan was a Muslim.

This story was first given a significant national platform by former Secretary of State Colin Powell, who referenced it when he endorsed Barack Obama for the presidency in 2008. The story resurfaced in July 2016 when Khizr and Ghazala Khan took center stage at the Democratic National Convention and invoked the memory of their dead son. Khizr Khan chastised Donald Trump, the Republican nominee, for demonizing Muslims and for proposing to ban them from the country. He asked Trump, "Have you ever been to Arlington Cemetery?" And then in the most memorable and heartbreaking statement of the evening if not the election, Khizr Khan raised his finger and his voice and proclaimed to Trump: "You have sacrificed nothing and no one."[7] Almost overnight, the entire nation was fixated on the death of a Muslim American soldier. Democrats and Republicans alike paused to acknowledge Muslims were among those who have fought and died for the United States.

Humayun Khan was not the first Muslim soldier to fight for the United States. Muslims, or those with a Muslim background, have served in or alongside the US Armed Forces since the Revolutionary War. Hundreds of soldiers on both sides of the Civil War had Muslim names. Some of the almost fourteen thousand Syrian Americans who fought in World War I were Muslims, as were upwards of 10 percent of the fifteen thousand Arab Americans who fought in World War II.[8]

It was only after World War II, however, that the military formally acknowledged Muslims as a distinct religious community. This is due in part to the efforts of Abdullah Igram, a Muslim American from Iowa who fought in the war. When he requested a dog tag with the letter "M" to indicate he was a Muslim, he was told that wasn't an option. The only options available to service members at the time were *P* for Protestant, *C* for Catholic, and *H* for Hebrew (Jewish). After the war, Igram wrote to the Secretary of the Army and to President Eisenhower to request these options be expanded to include a letter for Islam or Muslim. By the time of the Vietnam War, Islam was one of many options soldiers could choose from when deciding which religious affiliation to inscribe on their dog tags.[9]

According to the US Department of Defense, more than five thousand Muslims serve in the Armed Forces. The actual number is likely higher since almost half a million service members chose not to specify a religious preference when registering. One estimate suggests as many as fifteen thousand service members are Muslim.[10] Many of these individuals have served multiple tours in Afghanistan and Iraq as part of the War on Terror.

We must also keep in mind that Muslims have served the US military during the War on Terror in other ways, including as translators embedded with military units. Thousands of Iraqis, mostly Muslim, have worked in this capacity, helping US soldiers communicate with locals. In some cases, their efforts have made them targets of extremist groups who see interpreters as US spies. In appreciation for their efforts, organizations such as No One Left Behind have worked to help translators secure Special Immigrant Visas to the United States. This work became more difficult early in the Trump administration. Trump's initial executive order in January 2017 banned immigrants from seven Muslim-majority countries and shut the door on interpreters in Iraq from receiving visas.[11] The Trump administration later amended the ban to allow for Special Immigrant Visas in Iraq to proceed. But the executive order is a reminder of how easy it can be for powerful politicians to render Muslims invisible when it's expedient, including Muslims abroad who have assisted the US military.

Muslims in military service are not confined to the United States. Muslims have served in European militaries as well. This service also has a long history. More than four hundred thousand Muslim Indian soldiers fought for the British Empire in World War I, with almost nine hundred thousand Muslims fighting for the Allies.[12] Muslims have served in

European armies since then as well, from World War II to the wars in Afghanistan and Iraq.

The first British Muslim soldier to die in the War on Terror was Lance Corporal Jabron Hashmi. Hashmi's family had migrated to Britain from Pakistan when he was a child. He grew up in Birmingham and eventually joined the military. He died in southern Afghanistan in a Taliban attack. His brother, Zeeshan, said of Jabron: "He combined his love of Islam with the love of Britain."[13] Hashmi was one of about 320 Muslims serving in the British Armed Forces at the time. According to the Armed Forces Muslim Association, some 650 Muslims currently serve in the British Armed Forces, a relatively low percentage of the military.[14]

In France, the numbers are larger. According to one estimate, anywhere between 10 to 20 percent of the French army has a Muslim background.[15] Still, acceptance as a Muslim is not a given. When two sisters, Majda and Amina Belaroui, volunteered for France's military reserves after the 2016 terrorist attack in Nice, which killed 86 people, they met resistance from the recruiting center. Both were asked to remove their hijabs since France prohibits religious symbols in government spaces. Majda refused to do so and left, but Amina reluctantly agreed. The military was willing to accept the sisters on the condition they set aside their Muslim identities, or at least make these identities less visible.[16]

Challenges remain for Muslims serving in Western militaries, not least of which is the suspicion they sometimes face from other Muslims who see heavy-handed military responses to terrorism as contributing to the suffering of innocent people in Muslim-majority countries. Muslim service members are also the targets of taunting and hazing by fellow soldiers, often due to race and religion.[17] These challenges notwithstanding, what must be clear by now is that Muslims have played an integral role in military responses to terrorism since 9/11, in some cases sacrificing their lives for this cause.

Muslim Intelligence and Police Officers

The responsibility to root out terrorist cells and head off terrorist plots falls heavily on the intelligence and law enforcement agencies of the United States and Europe. Included in the ranks of these communities are Muslims.

It's difficult to sustain an in-depth discussion of Muslim contributions to the FBI or CIA, or to comparable agencies in Europe, mostly because we know very little about the number of Muslim employees in these agencies, much less what their day-to-day tasks are. Neither agency publishes data on the religious identities of its employees. The best you can do is look at the data each agency provides on the racial and ethnic composition of its employees. For example, in 2015, 1.1 percent of CIA officers had a Middle Eastern or Arab American background, and 4.5 percent had an Asian background.[18] What we don't know is how many employees with these backgrounds (or any other for that matter) identified as Muslims.

What we do know is that public appeals have been made

for these two agencies to recruit more Muslim agents and officers. Michael Leiter, the former director of the National Counterterrorism Center, told Chuck Todd on *Meet the Press* in 2014 that, in light of the rise of ISIS, it's clear the FBI doesn't have enough Muslim agents, nor does the FBI have enough agents who understand Islam.[19]

In December 2015, the CIA's deputy director gathered a group of Muslim employees to discuss Islamophobia in the wake of the San Bernardino attacks and Donald Trump's proposal to ban all Muslims from entering the country. CIA leaders noted this outreach to Muslim employees was important because the agency sees the contributions of these employees as "mission critical." For this reason, the agency took the unusual step of permitting some of its Muslim employees to speak to the *Washington Post* about their experience doing national security work.[20] The CIA wanted to signal to the broader public that Muslims are "one of us" and that its mission does not involve a hostile attack on Islam and those who practice it.

Muslims also play a significant role in local police departments. Of the thirty-six thousand NYPD officers, approximately a thousand are Muslim or have a Muslim background.[21] Other organizations in the United States represent significant numbers of police officers who have Muslim backgrounds, including the Arab American Police Association in Chicago and the Somali American Police Association in Minneapolis. In Britain, the National Association of Muslim Police represents some two thousand Muslims who serve in law enforcement in the country.[22] London has its own organization for Muslim officers in the Association of Muslim Police. In all of these cases, Muslim officers are among those who respond to reported terrorist threats or terrorist attacks.

Muslim police officers have received recognition from both superiors and politicians for their contributions in the fight against terrorism. Olly Martins, the former police and crime commissioner in Bedfordshire in Britain, oversaw a district with a high concentration of religious extremists. In a letter to Prime Minister David Cameron in 2015, Martins insisted: "Indeed, we have some fabulous local Muslim police officers in Bedfordshire that are the greatest weapon we have in the spread of extremism."[23]

In France, a Muslim police officer named Ahmed Merabet became a national hero after dying in a confrontation with the terrorists who attacked the Paris office of the satirical magazine *Charlie Hebdo* in January 2015. What's all the more poignant is that he gave his life in the line of duty and was shot at point blank range while defending a magazine that routinely ridiculed his religion. This was not lost on President François Hollande, who noted this sacrifice at Merabet's funeral when he bestowed France's highest award, the Legion of Honor, on the slain officer. Hollande called Merabet a symbol of the "diversity of France's forces of law and order."[24]

Muslims Cooperating with Law Enforcement

In March 2016, ISIS-inspired terrorists killed thirty-two people in Brussels. The day after the attacks, Donald Trump complained Muslims don't report trouble when they see it. "I don't know what it is. It's like they're protecting each other but they're really doing bad damage."[25] He leveled a similar accusation three months later after Omar Mateen shot and killed forty-nine people at the Pulse nightclub in Orlando. "They don't report them. For some reason the Muslim community does not report people like this."[26]

Trump's statements were false, and some high-profile folks called him on it. Britain's prime minister, at the time home secretary, Theresa May said Trump was "just plain wrong," at least when it came to her country.[27] FBI director James Comey insisted that "some of our most productive relationships with people who see things and tell us things happen to be Muslim."[28] Their statements echoed sentiments expressed years earlier by other prominent officials. This includes Eric Holder, the attorney general in the Obama administration, who insisted in 2010 that the "cooperation of Muslim and Arab-American communities has been absolutely essential in identifying, and preventing, terrorist threats."[29]

There's data to back up these observations. Charles Kurzman, a sociologist at the University of North Carolina, notes that from just after 9/11 through 2013, Muslims in the United States helped law enforcement identify 54 Muslim terrorism suspects or perpetrators out of a total of 188 individuals for whom the first tip was made public.[30] This means more than one quarter of Muslim terrorism suspects were made known to law enforcement by other Muslims. A different study from the Muslim Public Affairs Council confirms this trend. It found that Muslim Americans helped law enforcement officials disrupt one in three al-Qaeda terrorist plots from just after 9/11 through 2011.[31] It's important to point out these numbers don't capture the full extent of Muslim assistance to law enforcement since the data in both instances came from publicly available information. Not all tips are made known to the public.

Behind these numbers, we find real stories of Muslims cooperating with law enforcement in order to protect their communities from terrorist attacks. One example is the Muslim woman who tipped off the police about Abdelhamid Abaaoud, the mastermind of the Paris attacks in November 2015 that killed 130 people. She found out about Abaaoud and his plans for a second terrorist attack after accompanying Abaaoud's cousin to the terrorist's hiding place in a Paris suburb. She told journalists the reason she notified the police about Abaaoud's whereabouts and future plot was because she was a Muslim. Abaaoud's actions, she insisted, were contrary to Islam. Islam required he be brought to justice.[32] Abaaoud died in a police raid not long after the tip.

Mohammed Malik informed the FBI about the future Orlando terrorist, Omar Mateen, in 2014. Malik had gotten to know Mateen through a local mosque. When Mateen confided to Malik that he had developed an interest in the teachings of Anwar al-Awlaki, an al-Qaeda recruiter killed in a

2011 US drone strike, Malik reached out to the FBI. The FBI looked into Mateen after Malik's tip, but it didn't find enough to pursue an investigation.[33]

In the years leading up to an attack at a 2017 concert in Manchester that killed twenty-two people, members of the Muslim community reported the perpetrator, Salman Abedi, to law enforcement on multiple occasions. Didsbury Mosque banned Abedi from attending the mosque due to his extremist views. The mosque expressed its concerns about Abedi to Britain's Home Office. Friends and family members also brought Abedi's sympathetic views on terrorism to the attention of law enforcement.[34] The fact that Abedi still managed to carry out the attack had nothing to do with failures in the Muslim community.

It's time to reject unfounded accusations that Muslims are not reporting suspicious behavior. Many lives have been spared precisely because Muslims have been cooperative and proactive with law enforcement, while many more could have been spared had concerns from Muslims been given greater priority by the authorities.

Muslims Aiding Victims of Terrorism

Assumptions that Muslims are prone to sympathize with terrorists ignore the many instances in which Muslim communities visibly stand with the victims of terrorism. In some instances, they lead the way in charitable responses to those who have suffered from terrorist attacks.

Two notable ways in which Muslims have come to the

aid of victims in the aftermath of terrorist attacks have been through blood donations and fundraising. Immediately after 9/11, Muslims joined their fellow Americans in showing up to blood drives to help those injured in the attacks. Donating blood eventually turned into an annual event. To mark the tenth anniversary of the 9/11 attacks, Muslim communities organized blood drives across the United States as part of a campaign called Muslims for Life. These blood drives now take place every September to honor the victims of 9/11. The campaign references the Qur'an as justification for the blood drives: "If any saves a life it is as if he saves the lives of all mankind" (Q. 5:32). In the first four years alone, over one thousand blood drives were held, with almost forty thousand pints of blood collected.[35]

Muslims have contributed to blood drives after other terrorist attacks since 9/11. In Europe, Muslims lined up to give blood to help victims of the Paris and Brussels attacks. After the Orlando massacre, the Council on American-Islamic Relations (CAIR) urged Muslims to donate blood to help the victims, and Muslims obliged. This was all the more remarkable considering Muslims were observing Ramadan at the time and therefore were fasting.

In terms of fundraising, an initiative called Muslims United for San Bernardino raised just over $215,000 to help the families of the victims.[36] Muslims United for the Victims of Pulse Shooting raised over $100,000 for victims' families after the Orlando shootings.[37] Muslims United for London raised over $23,000 in just one day for victims of the Westminster terrorist attack.[38] In May 2017, Muslims started two fundraising campaigns in the aftermath of terrorist attacks: one to help families of the victims of the Manchester attack and one to assist the families of the heroic individuals killed on a Portland train while trying to protect two Muslim women from an anti-Muslim racist.[39] These and other initiatives drew inspiration from one verse in particular: "Repel evil with what is better" (Q. 41:34).

Muslims' fundraising efforts are not limited to attacks in which other Muslims are involved. When eight African American churches burned down in 2015, in some instances due to arson, a network of Muslim organizations raised over $100,000 to help the communities affected. They pointed out that the Qur'an insists on protecting all houses of worship, and not just mosques: "If God did not repel some people by means of others, many monasteries, churches, synagogues, and mosques, where God's name is much invoked, would have been destroyed" (Q. 22:40).[40]

Muslim Americans responded to the desecration of Jewish cemeteries in St. Louis and Philadelphia in 2017 by raising over $160,000 to repair the damaged headstones. The campaign invoked the Charter of Medina as a model for peaceful relationships between Medinan Jews and the earliest Muslim community. It also noted that according to Islamic tradition, the Prophet Muhammad once stood to pay respects to a Jewish funeral procession out of his belief the deceased was also a human soul, worthy of respect.[41]

Terrorists are in the business of violence and death. But

many Muslims have responded to the shedding of blood with the giving of blood, to the desecration of the sacred with the restoration of the sacred. They stand not with death and destruction but with love of neighbor and life itself.

* * *

We must be careful in telling the stories of Muslims taking action against terrorism not to fall into the good Muslim/bad Muslim trap. The good Muslim joins the military to fight in the War on Terror. The bad Muslim protests the War on Terror. The good Muslim works as an FBI agent. The bad Muslim condemns FBI surveillance of mosques as Islamophobic.

I'm not suggesting Muslims should be accepted as "good," or as "one of us," only after they wear a US or British military uniform, join the CIA or MI6, or can place "tipped off the police" or "gave blood to terrorism victims" on their resumes. In fact, Muslims continue to be viewed as outsiders and national security threats despite doing all of these things. It seems like no amount of patriotic or charitable deeds will enable Muslims to pay the requisite price for full admission into Western societies.

My more basic point, however, is that we shouldn't assume Muslims are dragging their feet in response to terrorism. Muslims are doing lots of things, some of which involve actions typically hailed by their harshest critics as essential in the fight against terrorism. And there's far more to what Muslims are doing in this fight than can be covered here, including serving in a variety of government agencies, working for charitable and human rights organizations, and mentoring other Muslims in their local communities.

We can debate whether some of the actions described above, such as military intervention, are helpful to Muslims or to the overall effort to counter terrorism. I, for one, have plenty of criticisms of the Iraq War and how it created the conditions that gave rise to ISIS. The Iraq War did far more harm than good, to Muslims and non-Muslims alike. But what shouldn't be debated is whether Muslims are responding to terrorism with actions. They are. Sometimes they put their lives on the line to do so. And it falls on those of us in the non-Muslim majority to do what we can to bear witness to their deeds.

Notes

1. "Mission," FY 2004–2009 Department of State and USAID Strategic Plan, US Department of State, http://tinyurl.com/ydaae8gw.

2. "Confronting Fear: Islamophobia and Its Impact in the United States," Council on American-Islamic Relations and the U.C. Berkeley Center for Race and Gender, 2016, PDF, https://tinyurl.com/yc7h7vgd.

3. John Harkinson, "Trump Campaign CEO Was a Big Promoter of Anti-Muslim Extremists," *Mother Jones*, September 15, 2016, https://tinyurl.com/y6wbodvz.

4. Martin Luther King Jr., "Letter from a Birmingham Jail," African Studies Center—University of Pennsylvania, April 16, 1963, http://tinyurl.com/y9xqb2xn.

5. Daniel F. Baltrusaitis, *Coalition Politics and the Iraq War: Determinants of Choice* (Boulder, CO: Lynne Rienner, 2010), 150.

6. Gareth Winrow, "Turkey: Recalcitrant Ally," in *The Iraq War: Causes and Consequences*, ed. Rick Fawn and Raymond Hinnebusch (Boulder, CO: Lynne Rienner, 2006), 197–208.

7. "Full Text: Khizr Khan's Speech to the 2016 Democratic National Convention," ABC News, August 1, 2016, https://tinyurl.com/ycqrvngx.

8. Edward E. Curtis IV, *Muslim Americans in the Military: Centuries of Service* (Bloomington: Indiana University Press, 2016), 24, 29.

9. Lily Rothman, "The Khan Family and American History's Hidden Muslim Soldiers," *Time*, August 3, 2016, https://tinyurl.com/guxxg3z.

10. Curtis, *Muslim Americans*, 69.

11. Matt Zeller, "Trump Shuts the Door on Men and Women Who Have Sacrificed for America," *Washington Post*, January 28, 2017, https://tinyurl.com/ybklnwza.

12. Mary Atkinson, "Britain's Forgotten Army of Muslims Fighting in WWI," Middle East Eye, March 13, 2016, https://tinyurl.com/yaea9rna.

13. Jacqueline Maley and Sam Jones, "Jabron Hashmi, the British Muslim Soldier Killed Fighting the Taliban," *The Guardian*, July 3, 2006, https://tinyurl.com/ycflufzo.

14. "About Us," Armed Forces Muslim Association, http://afma.org.uk/about-us/.

15. Collette Davidson, "Why French Military May Be More Tolerant of Muslims Than French Society," *The Christian Science Monitor*, March 1, 2016, https://tinyurl.com/y9l2xhac.

16. Daniel Estrin, "French Army Asks Citizens to Enlist—But No Muslim Headscarves, Please," NPR, July 26, 2016, https://tinyurl.com/ydyf6dqd.

17. Michelle Sandhoff, *Service in a Time of Suspicion: Experiences of Muslims Serving in the U.S. Military Post-9/11* (Iowa City: University of Iowa Press, 2017); Janet Reitman, "How the Death of a Muslim Recruit Revealed a Culture of Brutality in the Marines," *New York Times Magazine*, July 6, 2017, https://tinyurl.com/y8yzsnnq.

18. Central Intelligence Agency, *Director's Diversity in Leadership Study: Overcoming Barriers to Advancement*, 2015, 22, PDF, https://tinyurl.com/y8onwtjx.

19. "Meet the Press Transcript—October 26, 2014," NBC News, October 26, 2014, https://tinyurl.com/y7w84ew6.

20. Missy Ryan, "As the Nation Debates the Place of Islam, the CIA's Muslim Officers Fight Terrorism," *Washington Post*, June 21, 2016, https://tinyurl.com/yagfdsba.

21. "Muslim NYPD Officer on Advice He Gives Bullied Daughter," CBS News, August 23, 2016, https://tinyurl.com/yd65h6k4.

22. Büşra Akin Dinçer, "Muslim Police: A Bridge between Different Cultures," *Daily Sabah*, March 20, 2015, https://tinyurl.com/y8hrwd6w.

23. Graeme Demianyk, "Police Commissioner Who Says Muslim Police Officers Are 'Greatest Weapons' in Tackling Extremism Warns Prime Minister against Cuts," *Huffington Post*, November 19, 2015, https://tinyurl.com/ycspmcx4.

24. Kim Willsher, "Charlie Hebdo Attack: Fallen Policeman Ahmed Merabet Buried in Bobigny," *The Guardian*, January 13, 2015, https://tinyurl.com/yahdfog8.

25. Guy Faulconbridge and William Schomberg, "Trump Says Muslims Not Doing Enough to Prevent Attacks," *Reuters*, March 23, 2016, https://tinyurl.com/ya5fzsj8.

26. David Alexander, "Trump, on CNN, Faults Muslim Community for Not Reporting People Like Orlando Shooter," *Reuters*, June 13, 2016, https://tinyurl.com/yczgy9rk.

27. Faulconbridge and Schomberg, "Trump Says Muslims Not Doing Enough."

28. Kristina Cooke and Joseph Ax, "U.S. Officials Say American Muslims Do Report Extremist Threats," *Reuters*, June 16, 2016, https://tinyurl.com/y9hdchdm.

29. "Attorney General Eric Holder Speaks at the Muslim Advocates' Annual Dinner," The United States Department of Justice, December 10, 2010, https://tinyurl.com/yagj9gv2.

30. Charles Kurzman, "Muslim-American Terrorism in 2013," University of North Carolina, February 5, 2014, 4, PDF, https://tinyurl.com/yda7co32.

31. See Muslim Public Affairs Council, *Data on Post-911 Terrorism in the United States*, June 2012, 12–13, PDF, https://tinyurl.com/y9foj5eh.

32. Greg Miller and Souad Mekhennet, "One Woman Helped the

Mastermind of the Paris Attacks. The Other Turned Him In," *Washington Post*, April 10, 2016, https://tinyurl.com/ybrdkcwk.

33. Mohammed A. Malik, "I Reported Omar Mateen to the FBI. Trump Is Wrong that Muslims Don't Do Our Part," *Washington Post*, June 20, 2016, https://tinyurl.com/ybluqf2u.

34. Robert Mendick, "Security Services Missed Five Opportunities to Stop Manchester Bomber," *The Telegraph*, May 25, 2017, https://tinyurl.com/y86659cp.

35. Muslims for Life, available online at www.muslimsforlife.org.

36. "Muslims United for San Bernardino Families," LaunchGood, https://tinyurl.com/y73vtjxe.

37. "Muslims United for Victims of Pulse Shooting," LaunchGood, https://tinyurl.com/ybyd6y52.

38. "Muslims United for London," LaunchGood, https://tinyurl.com/y7adp79w.

39. "Muslim Engagement and Development," JustGiving, https://tinyurl.com/y95s6pff; "Muslims Unite for Portland Heroes," LaunchGood, https://tinyurl.com/y84g7p83.

40. "Rebuild with Love: Rebuild Black Churches and Support Victims of Arson across the South," LaunchGood, https://tinyurl.com/ybod8gcj.

41. "Muslims Unite to Repair Jewish Cemetery," LaunchGood, https://tinyurl.com/y7akdytn.

PART III

Diverting Attention
from Western Violence

5

The Sins of the Fathers

I'm not a big fan of the National Prayer Breakfast. I have always been suspicious of politicians putting their piety on display. It comes across as an insincere ploy to get votes from people of faith. It also brings to mind Jesus's admonition against praying in order to be seen and admired by others.

Many politicians and faith leaders don't share my opinion of the prayer breakfast. On the first Thursday in February, they ceremoniously gather in Washington to showcase their faith for the media and the American public. A less cynical view is they are setting aside partisan divisions for one day to celebrate the spiritual ties that bind the nation together. Perhaps. But I'm still not convinced that a televised prayer event spotlighting clergy, congressional representatives, and the commander-in-chief is capable of transcending political expediency.

My skepticism normally prompts me to tune out the prayer breakfast. But in 2015, I was in a different mood. This time,

I made sure to tune in. I wanted to hear what President Obama had to say. What changed my mind was ISIS. ISIS was the new global threat weighing on everyone's mind, and I wanted to hear how our theologian-in-chief was going to make sense of this threat from the perspective of his Christian faith. I held out hope that the political setting wouldn't prompt him to pander to the American public and engage in simplistic anecdotes pitting civilized Christians against backward Muslims.

Obama didn't disappoint. He exercised his theological chops and reflected on religion's potential to inspire love and hatred, peace and violence. In addressing Islam, his initial focus was on the recent atrocities committed in its name from Pakistan to Paris. He took particular aim at ISIS's "unspeakable acts of barbarism," including its persecution of Yazidis and its recourse to rape as a tool for war.[1]

Then he turned his attention to Christianity. He urged his audience to "remember that during the Crusades and the Inquisition, people committed terrible deeds in the name of Christ," adding that "slavery and Jim Crow all too often was justified in the name of Christ." The sinful tendency to distort religion for violent ends was not unique to one place or one religion. Humility, not hubris, was in order when tackling the problem of religiously framed violence.

I loved his speech. But I was in the minority. Religious leaders, politicians, and mainstream journalists went on the attack. They chastised Obama for his insensitivity to Christians and for his failure to keep his focus on "radical Islamic terrorism."

Russell Moore, president of the Southern Baptist Ethics and Religious Liberty Commission, called Obama's comments "an unfortunate attempt at a wrongheaded moral comparison."[2] Governor Bobby Jindal of Louisiana mocked the president for giving an irrelevant history lesson, assuring him that the "medieval Christian threat is under control."[3] A journalist I respect greatly, NBC's Andrea Mitchell, scolded the president for invoking the Crusades and digging into the past. In light of ISIS's current atrocities, "you don't lean over backwards to be philosophical about the sins of the fathers."[4]

Obama's great crime in all of this was to tell the truth. He acknowledged unjust violence targeting civilians or inflicting terror on the innocent is a human problem, not confined to any one people, religion, or nation. He diverted attention away from violent Muslims to address violent Christians. It was a brief detour—two sentences to be exact—but enough of one to cast doubt that Muslim extremists have a monopoly on barbarity and bloodshed.

Obama was not supposed to tell this story. None of us are. I once spoke at a monastery and noted the kinds of atrocities committed by ISIS—rape, torture, genocide—have been committed by Western Christians too, and not just in the distant past. It didn't go over well. One of the monks wrote to me afterward to express his concern that I was blaming Christians for violence instead of keeping my focus on violent Muslims.

He made it clear that Christians doing violent things was not on the table for discussion.

Telling the story of Western violence and the role of Christians in it will not endear you to many. But the fact that there's so much resistance to this story is an indication there are truths in our history we must confront, skeletons in our national and religious closets that must see the light of day. It's time to tell this story and to wrestle with these truths, difficult and painful as it may be.

The story I will tell is suggestive, not exhaustive. It's the story of how unjust violence has shaped our history going back to the Middle Ages, and how this violence informs national identities in Europe and the United States to this day. It's also the story of how categories of violence assumed to be endemic to Islam feature prominently in our history. Holy wars and inquisitions, the subject of this chapter, illustrate this point. Fighting wars and persecuting heretics in the name of God characterize extremist groups like ISIS. But they characterize Western Christians at various points in history too.

We need help in remembering that unspeakable violence is not just something "they" do but factors into the collective histories of all peoples. Sadly, many of us don't know our own history of violence, or we only know sanitized versions of it that reinforce a sense of Western and Christian superiority. Focusing attention on Western violence is a humbling exercise. It collapses the false dichotomy pitting a "violent Islam" against a "peaceful West." It also wards off the temptation to project onto Muslim communities our own sins of commission and omission when it comes to violence.

At a more basic level, we must face the truth about ourselves. We are who we are today because of a long history of unjust violence, much of it performed within a Christian framework. This violence gave birth to modern Western nations, sustained systemic injustices, and paved the way for Western global domination. If we wish to start a new chapter of history, one characterized not by war and terrorism but by reconciliation and healing between and within nations and religions, we must own this truth. As James Baldwin noted: "Not everything that is faced can be changed, but nothing can be changed until it is faced."[5]

Crusades and Holy War

A good place to start when facing uncomfortable truths about Western violence is holy war. Holy war refers to war ordained or mandated by God. Those on the other side of the conflict, combatants and noncombatants, are enemies of God and of the one true religion. Other motives for fighting, whether economic or political, may come into play, but holy warriors depend heavily on religion to sanctify their cause.

We often think of holy war as primitive, the relic of a bygone era. Only jihadists still fight holy wars, invoking God to justify their bloodshed. But as we'll see, holy war is more integral to Western history than is often assumed.

The Crusades stand out as the quintessential example of Christians going to battle on the conviction that it was God's will. The Crusades were a series of European military campaigns, sanctioned and promoted by the Catholic Church, from the eleventh through thirteenth centuries. Their main purpose was to conquer and retake territory from Muslims in Palestine. Pope Urban II ordered the First Crusade in 1095 in response to the Byzantine emperor's call for assistance to fight off invading Muslim Turks.

The First Crusade focused on capturing Jerusalem. In 1099, Christian armies succeeded in this task and went on to establish other kingdoms. Holding on to Jerusalem proved difficult, however, as the city fell to the great Muslim general Saladin less than a century later. Additional crusades ensued, often prompted by Muslim conquests of territory held by Christian rulers. Most of these crusades failed. By the end of the thirteenth century, the last great European stronghold in the region had fallen into Muslim hands.

All of these crusading battles reflected a basic theological premise: Christians must wipe out Muslims because "God wills it." Pope Urban II did not mince words about God's hatred for Muslims. He described Muslims as "an accursed race, a race utterly alienated from God." Christians were obligated "to exterminate this vile race from our lands."[6]

Violent language translated into violent actions. When Christians attacked Jerusalem during the First Crusade, they massacred some thirty thousand people in the span of three days. The invading army spared no Muslim, male or female. A prominent chronicler of the First Crusade observed: "Men rode in blood up to their knees and bridle reins. Indeed, it was a just and splendid judgment of God that this place should be filled with the blood of unbelievers."[7] The body count was so high that the crusaders didn't know what to do with all of the bodies. Six months later, an overwhelming stench emanating from decaying corpses was on hand to meet visitors to the city.

Muslims were not the only victims. The Christian army rounded up the Jews of Jerusalem into the synagogue and massacred them. In fact, the Crusades set off a wave of violence against Jews, understandable given that many Crusaders lumped Jews in with Muslims as enemies of the faith. In 1096, a German crusading army attacked Jewish communities in the Rhineland region, killing between four and eight thousand Jews. Some Jews avoided death only after submitting to forced conversions.

Though holy war reached its zenith with the Crusades, Europe witnessed other conflicts in which participants saw themselves fighting (or encouraging others to fight) to fulfill God's will. Ferdinand II, emperor of Germany during the Thirty Years' War (1618–1648), viewed battles against Protestants as ordained by God. In the lead-up to the English Civil War (1642–1651), Protestant clergy such as William Gouge heralded wars "extraordinarily made by express charge from God."[8] Giuseppe Mazzini, a nineteenth-century Italian revolutionary, believed the quest to unify Italy was a holy struggle, an effort to realize God's plan for an independent nation.

Romanticized notions of the Crusades also took a firm hold

in nineteenth-century art and literature. King Louis-Philippe of France opened a series of rooms known as the Hall of Crusades in the Palace of Versailles in 1843. Over 120 paintings dedicated to the glories of the Crusades and France's military contributions to them were on full display. Sir Walter Scott set four of his novels, including *Ivanhoe* (1819), to the Crusades, while William Wordsworth devoted four sonnets to them.

Nineteenth-century Europeans invoked the Crusades for different reasons. For some, it was to reclaim Europe's Christian past in the wake of rising secularization. For others, it was to lend legitimacy to colonialist enterprises in the "Orient," or to encourage nationalist fervor. Whatever the reason, it's clear modern European identity took shape not by snubbing this violent history but by cozying up to it.

In America, appeals to holy war began with the Puritan settlers. They saw themselves as chosen by God and destined to be "a city upon a hill." They characterized their militaristic encounters with indigenous peoples as evidence of God's providential will. As one English author put it during King Phillip's War in 1676: "God himself hath sent from Heaven and saved us . . . by Wasting the Indians with Sickness, Starving them through want of Provisions, Leaving them to their own Divisions, Taking away their Spirits, putting the Dread of us upon them."[9]

In the Revolutionary War, revolutionaries not only beseeched God for protection but insisted God was a revolutionary too. One Connecticut minister proclaimed: "God

Almighty, with all the powers of heaven, are on our side. Great numbers of angels, no doubt, are encamping round our coast, for our defense and protection."[10] George Washington encouraged his troops "to implore the blessings of heaven upon the means used for our safety and defense."[11]

The conviction that God was on "our side" also took root during the Civil War. One Northern minister saw the Union army as God's instrument in purging the nation of its sins so that it would once again be "a city set on a hill, whose light cannot be hid." Confederate supporters also believed God was on their side, even when things didn't go well on the battlefield.[12] One Episcopal priest interpreted General Stonewall Jackson's accidental death at the hands of his own soldiers as an act of God, a result of Southerners trusting "too much in *him* and too little in *God.*"[13] Abraham Lincoln heard these conflicting appeals from a divided nation. While he didn't deny God's involvement in war, he did warn against certain knowledge of divine providence: "In the present civil war it is quite possible that God's purpose is something quite different from the purpose of either party."[14]

We might expect that by the twentieth century, the full rush of modernity would have put an end to warfare fought in defense of God's cause. Not so. Holy war rhetoric flourished in World War I. The rector of the Church of the Epiphany in Washington believed not only that "it is God who has summoned us to this war" but that the war was "in the profoundest and truest sense a Holy War."[15] The famed Congregationalist minister Lyman Abbott viewed the war as "a crusade to make this world a home in which God's children can live in peace and safety."[16] Some pushed these holy war doctrines to an extreme, with the Anglican bishop of London insisting it was a divine duty to kill all Germans, "to kill the good as well as the bad, to kill the young as well as the old, to kill those who have shown kindness to our wounded as well as those fiends."[17]

Holy war rhetoric found a home on the other side of the conflict as well. Kaiser Wilhelm of Germany was convinced England was in league with Satan and the war was a fight against ultimate evil. Dietrich Vorwerk, a German pastor, rewrote the Lord's Prayer as a call to holy war, beseeching God to "help us in the holy war," to "forgive each bullet and each blow that misses the mark," and to "lead us not into temptation of letting our wrath be too gentle in carrying out Thy divine judgment."[18]

Few European or American wars of the twentieth century matched World War I in its religious fervor. One is much harder pressed to find abundant holy war rhetoric, for example, during World War II, though prominent leaders still found ways to inject God and Christianity into the conflict. We see this in Franklin Roosevelt's 1941 radio address, just before the United States' entry into the war: "Today the whole world is divided between human slavery and human freedom—between pagan brutality and the Christian ideal."[19] Roosevelt left little doubt as to which side God's providential protection could be found.

The idea that God actively participates and chooses sides in war persists in our post-9/11 world. Just days after the 9/11 attacks, Reverend Jerry Falwell explained on television that what happened was a result of God's will. God was punishing the nation because of its tolerance for a whole host of enemies who have secularized America: the American Civil Liberties Union, abortionists, pagans, feminists, and gays and lesbians. "I point the finger in their face and say, 'You helped this happen,'" insisted Falwell.[20] More was to come if God "continues to lift the curtain and allow the enemies of America to give us probably what we deserve."[21]

President Bush rejected Falwell's theological rationale. The fault for 9/11 lay solely with the terrorists. Yet Bush made it clear God had a part to play in the War on Terror: "Freedom and fear have always been at war, and we know that God is not neutral between them."[22] Bush did court controversy for flirting with holy war doctrines. Not long after the attacks, he stated that "this crusade" to bring to justice those responsible for planning and organizing the attacks was going to take a while. Friends and foes alike thought Bush was calling for a holy war. Bush later backed off this language, but the crusading reference, along with his other Christian allusions and his categorizing of certain countries as the "Axis of Evil," gave the conflict a persistent holy war vibe.

What we have here are snapshots of very complex conflicts in which participants invoked a variety of rationales to make sense of their cause. But without a doubt, the language of holy war has endured well beyond the Middle Ages and has become very much a part of the Western vocabulary of violence.

Inquisitions and Heresy Trials

Since ISIS first gained international attention in 2014, its persecution of religious minorities has been front and center in the news. ISIS has accused Christians, Yazidis, and Shiʻa Muslims of heresy. Such accusations form the basis of widespread violence and persecution against these communities in ISIS-controlled regions of Syria and Iraq.

The persecution of religious minorities and heretics has a history in Islam that predates ISIS. But this is no great observation. Efforts to root out heresy and to suppress religious minorities have a long history in Christianity as well. While crusades were typically launched against external enemies, inquisitions and heresy trials took aim at internal enemies.

In medieval Christianity, the institution designed to address the crime of heresy was the Inquisition. In the thirteenth century, Pope Gregory IX called for special tribunals, made up of Franciscan and Dominican judges or inquisitors, to oversee the inquisitorial process. Inquisitors questioned those accused of heresy and interviewed witnesses who might shed light on the case. Inquisitors had two purposes: to discover whether the accused was guilty of holding unorthodox views and to ferret out of the accused what they knew about the unorthodox beliefs and practices of family members, friends, and neighbors.

As the Inquisition unfolded, techniques were employed to

elicit confessions. Torture was one technique, though confessions based on torture alone were insufficient. The accused had to repeat the confession outside the torture chamber. Those who confessed often received lifelong imprisonment. Heretics who relapsed or who refused to recant were turned over to the secular authorities for capital punishment. The most common form of execution was burning at the stake. The reason for burning heretics was to reduce the body to ashes in order to prevent it from being resurrected upon Christ's return.[23] Because these burnings were public spectacles, they also discouraged others from flirting with heresy.

Other inquisitions followed the medieval Inquisition, most notably the Spanish Inquisition. It began under Isabella of Castile and Ferdinand of Aragon in 1478, formalized by a decree from Pope Sixtus IV. The driving force behind the Spanish Inquisition was anxiety over first Jews and then Muslims who had converted to Christianity. Jewish conversions dated back to the fourteenth century as Jews sought to cope with outbreaks of persecution in the wake of significant economic and political upheavals. Between 1391 and 1415, a little more than half of Spanish Jews underwent baptism.[24] By the fifteenth century, Jewish converts were referred to as New Christians or *conversos* to distinguish them from other Jews. However, suspicions about the true religious convictions of *conversos* lingered. Both political and religious elites feared the very presence of Jews in Spain might tempt *conversos* to revert back to Judaism.

The Spanish Inquisition's initial purpose was to strengthen

Christian orthodoxy by eliminating obstacles to the assimilation of *conversos*. For this reason, Isabella and Ferdinand ordered the expulsion of Jews from Spain in 1492. Between fifty and one hundred thousand Jews left Spain. Most settled in the Ottoman Empire, while others moved to Portugal, Italy, or North Africa.[25]

The desire to impose Christian orthodoxy also led to the forced conversions of Muslims. These conversions began already in the early sixteenth century. Muslim converts were known as *moriscos*. Those who didn't convert were expelled. Tensions between *moriscos* and "Old Christians" intensified in the course of the century. In 1609, King Philip III decreed the expulsion of all *moriscos*, resulting in the departure of some three hundred thousand people.[26] Combined with earlier expulsions of Jews and Muslims, this decree helped "cleanse" Spain of those populations that might tarnish the true Christian faith. By the eighteenth century, much of the work of the Spanish Inquisition was done, though the institution remained in force until the nineteenth century.

Forced conversions and expulsions are themselves violent acts. But the Spanish Inquisition inflicted other forms of violence upon its victims. Torture was one means of eliciting a confession, as it had been during the medieval Inquisition. Such torture included a procedure similar to waterboarding in which a cloth was inserted into the accused's mouth and water was poured into it to simulate drowning. The rack was another torture technique. This involved binding the wrists and ankles of the accused with ropes and then incrementally tightening the ropes by twisting them.

The most severe fate awaiting accused heretics beyond the torture chamber or the trial was death, with several thousand people executed in the course of the Spanish Inquisition, often by burning at the stake.[27] Many more thousands received punishments that included public whipping, forced labor, or imprisonment. And this is only a fraction of the tens of thousands of individuals that were put on trial under suspicion of lapsing from the Christian faith.

The Spanish Inquisition concerned itself mostly with those of Jewish and Muslim backgrounds, but there were instances in which Protestant heretics were targeted as well. The attention given to Protestants, while comparatively small, was a reflection of the larger upheavals that swept much of sixteenth-century Europe as a result of the Reformation. The Reformation was a theological movement that began in Germany in 1517 and extended into the seventeenth century. It generated a deep rift within Western Christianity between Roman Catholicism and Protestantism.

The Reformation spawned its own heresy trials and executions, both in Catholic and Protestant regions. Somewhere in the neighborhood of three thousand people were executed for heresy in Europe between 1520 and 1565. Approximately two-thirds of the victims were Anabaptists, members of a Protestant movement that rejected infant baptism and the state's authority over the church.[28] In Germany, Switzerland, the Netherlands, and Belgium, Anabaptists met horrible fates, including death by drowning, burning at the stake, and beheading.

Other victims of Reformation executions included Huguenots in France and Protestant dissidents in Queen Mary's England (that's how she became known as "Bloody Mary"). Some heresy executions received lots of publicity. Such was the case with Michael Servetus, who was burned at the stake in John Calvin's Geneva in 1553 for denying the Trinity and rejecting infant baptism.

The number of heresy executions in Reformation Europe, while tragic, pales in comparison to the number of people put to death for witchcraft during roughly the same time period. According to conservative estimates, at least fifty thousand people were executed, and twice that number tried, for witchcraft.[29] Common forms of execution included burning at the stake and hanging. Both Protestant and Catholic regions participated in the witch craze, with the most intense activity in Germany and Switzerland.

Like other forms of inquisitions and heresy hunts, witch persecutions involved the application of torture to extract confessions from the accused. Torture methods included the use of *pinniewinks*, or thumbscrews, to crush fingers, and the *strappado*, in which the victim's hands were tied behind their back and attached to a pulley from which they were lifted off the ground and jerked violently, often resulting in joint dislocation. More severe forms of torture included mutilating breasts and genitals and setting alcohol-soaked skin on fire.

We can't understand the witch craze apart from theology.

For much of the Middle Ages, the link between magic and the devil was loose. Plenty of medieval Christians dabbled in magic. Some magic was intended for good, some not. Witches were those who practiced *maleficia*, or magic aimed at harming others. Beginning in the fourteenth and fifteenth centuries, the church began to connect witches with satanic activity. The belief developed that witches made a pact with the devil; that's where they got the power to do *maleficia*. But if they were in league with Satan, they couldn't also be in a relationship with God. They must be treated as heretics.

While both men and women met a tragic end during the witch craze, the overwhelming majority of those tried and convicted were women. This was no coincidence. The theology that defined witchcraft as a heresy also rationalized the notion that women were far more likely than men to succumb to this heresy. Most theologians saw women as the weaker sex, more bodily and less rational. Women were no match for the devil, who had a track record going back to Eve of appealing to women's lesser nature to make them do things that undermined God's will.

Such views were on full display in the most prominent witch-hunt manual of the time, *Malleus Maleficarum* (*The Hammer of the Witches*). This manual connected women's sexual nature with their propensity toward evil, noting that witchcraft "comes from carnal lust, which is in women insatiable."[30] The manual viewed women's tendency to waver in the faith, a casualty of their weaker intellect, as another reason for their susceptibility toward witchcraft. Such opinions about women were commonplace, and women paid a much heavier and lethal price as a result.

* * *

The days of inquisitions and witch trials are long past. Yet the contemporary religious landscape of Europe—including the confessional divide between a Protestant north and a Catholic south, government regulations of religious identity and expression, and the ongoing struggle to accept religious diversity—makes little sense without taking this history into account. As for holy wars, evidence from both sides of the Atlantic suggests these are not relics of the Middle Ages. The bloody conflicts characterizing our modern history, from civil wars to world wars to wars on terror, continue to reflect a collective mentality that places the divine clearly on one side (usually ours). They also constitute a larger story that raises important questions about which victims of Western and Christian violence we remember, and how we remember them.

Notes

1. The full text for President Obama's 2015 prayer breakfast speech can be found here: "Remarks by the President at National Prayer Breakfast," The White House Office of the Press Secretary, February 5, 2015, http://tinyurl.com/y82dmafy.
2. Juliet Eilperin, "Critics Pounce after Obama talks Crusades, Slavery at Prayer Breakfast," *Washington Post*, February 5, 2015, http://tinyurl.com/ybxfw68v.

3. Jose A. DelReal and Katie Zezima, "Jindal: 'The Medieval Christian Threat Is Under Control, Mr. President,'" *Washington Post*, February 6, 2015, http://tinyurl.com/y98crkbg.

4. Ian Schwartz, "Andrea Mitchell Rips Obama Prayer Speech: After a Pilot Is Burned, 'You Don't Lean Over Backward and Be Philosophical,'" *Real Clear Politics*, February 8, 2015, http://tinyurl.com/y8xk4qzr.

5. James Baldwin, "As Much Truth as One Can Bear," in *The Cross of Redemption: Uncollected Writings*, ed. Randall Kenan (New York: Vintage, 2011), 34.

6. Lloyd Steffen, "Religion and Violence in Christian Traditions," in *The Oxford Handbook of Religion and Violence*, ed. Mark Juergensmeyer, Margo Kitts, and Michael Jerryson (Oxford: Oxford University Press, 2013), 112.

7. Karen Armstrong, *Fields of Blood: Religion and the History of Violence* (New York: Alfred A. Knopf, 2014), 214.

8. James Turner Johnson, *Ideology, Reason, and the Limitation of War: Religious and Secular Concepts, 1200–1740* (Princeton: Princeton University Press, 1975), 119.

9. Andrew R. Murphy and Elizabeth Hanson, "From King Philip's War to September 11: Religion, Violence, and the American Way," in *From Jeremiad to Jihad: Religion, Violence, and America*, ed. John D. Carlson and Jonathan H. Ebel (Berkeley: University of California Press, 2012), 33.

10. James P. Byrd, *Sacred Scripture, Sacred War: The Bible and the American Revolution* (Oxford: Oxford University Press, 2013), 1.

11. Byrd, *Sacred Scripture, Sacred War*, 42.

12. Murphy and Hanson, "From King Philip's War," 36–37.

13. Daniel W. Stowell, "Stonewall Jackson and the Providence of God," in *Religion and the American Civil War*, ed. Randall M. Miller, Harry S. Stout, and Charles Reagan Wilson (New York: Oxford University Press, 1998), 192.

14. Murphy and Hanson, "From King Philip's War," 38.

15. Philip Jenkins, *The Great and Holy War: How World War I Became a Religious Crusade* (New York: HarperOne, 2014), 10.

16. Jenkins, *Great and Holy War*, 95.

17. Jenkins, *Great and Holy War*, 71.

18. Jenkins, *Great and Holy War*, 11.

19. Stephen H. Webb, "American Providence, American Violence," in Carlson and Ebel, *From Jeremiad to Jihad*, 101.

20. Laurie Goodstein, "Falwell: Blame Abortionists, Feminists and Gays," *The Guardian*, September 19, 2001, http://tinyurl.com/yb2no9gz.

21. Murphy and Hanson, "From King Philip's War," 40.

22. Murphy and Hanson, "From King Philip's War," 41.

23. Jennifer Kolpacoff Deane, *A History of Medieval Heresy and Inquisition* (Lanham: Rowman & Littlefield, 2011), 95.

24. Joseph Pérez, *The Spanish Inquisition: A History*, trans. Janet Lloyd (New Haven: Yale University Press, 2005), 12.

25. Pérez, *Spanish Inquisition*, 36.

26. Toby Green, *Inquisition: The Reign of Fear* (New York: St. Martin's Press, 2009), 188.

27. Henry Kamen, *The Spanish Inquisition: A Historical Revision* (New Haven: Yale University Press, 2014), 68.

28. William Monter, "Heresy Executions in Reformation Europe, 1520–1565," in *Tolerance and Intolerance in the European Reformation*, ed. Ole Peter Grell and Bob Scribner (Cambridge: Cambridge University Press, 1996), 49.

29. Malcolm Gaskill, *Witchcraft: A Very Short Introduction* (Oxford: Oxford University Press, 2010), 69; Alan Charles Kors and Edward Peters, "Introduction: The Problem of European Witchcraft," in *Witchcraft in Europe, 400–1700: A Documentary History*, ed. Alan Charles Kors and Edward Peters (Philadelphia: University of Pennsylvania Press, 2001), 17.

30. Heinrich Kramer and Jacob Sprenger, "The *Malleus Maleficarum*," in Kors and Peters, *Witchcraft in Europe*, 188.

6

A Written Memorial

I visited the 9/11 Memorial Museum in New York City just a month after it opened. It was an overwhelming experience. The museum connects you emotionally and physically to the site of the World Trade Center, where over 2,700 victims perished. Detailed maps pinpoint where you are standing in relation to the original buildings. Video footage of the planes penetrating the towers engulfs you in one room as sound recordings of frantic 911 calls play in the background. The steel frames of the original buildings invite you to touch them, to feel a piece of America's tragic history.

The most powerful part of the museum was a section dedicated to telling the stories of the dead. I sat in a dark room while one by one, photos of individual victims were projected onto a wall. They were accompanied by audio commentary from a loved one telling an anecdote about the person. In the time I sat in this space, I "met" all sorts of people: a newlywed, an art aficionado, a fan of Norse mythology, a former high school jock. All of them perished on that fateful day in 2001. I remember one woman reminiscing about the sister she lost. She wavered between laughter and tears as she recalled how her sister loved to do Barbara Streisand imitations. "Now *that* sounds like a fun person," I thought. What struck me about all of the commentaries was that none were vengeful or angry. They came across as profound reflections on what it means to go on living life with wounds that never fully heal.

I left the museum feeling more connected to the pain, suffering, and loss that marks that day and indeed the human condition. But in retrospect, it's clear the museum directed my emotional energy to the pain of some but not others. From a broader perspective, there are far more victims of the 9/11 attacks than the almost three thousand people killed that day, many of them civilian casualties of the subsequent War on Terror in Afghanistan and Iraq. But there is no room in the 9/11 Memorial Museum dedicated to their memories. And then there are the prisoners and detainees tortured by or with the help of the United States in response to the 9/11 attacks. But there is no museum exhibit on torture or CIA black sites, no place to go and hear the stories of those who endured forced sodomy or waterboarding. I was not meant to think about these victims. In fact, I know of no memorial or museum dedicated to the victims of torture from the War on Terror.

There's a pattern in America when it comes to forgetting or erasing the pain of those who have suffered from unjust violence at our nation's hands. Take, for instance, the victims of racial violence. I'm from the South, home to some of the most disturbing and tragic episodes in American history: slavery, lynchings, and Jim Crow. But when I visit the South, I'm hard pressed to find the equivalent of a 9/11 Memorial Museum devoted to the unjust suffering of Africans and African Americans.

The good news is that we're starting to see efforts to remedy the lack of memorials devoted to victims of racial violence. A former slave plantation in Louisiana, the Whitney Plantation, opened a museum dedicated entirely to slavery in 2014. It joined the ranks of a small group of museums whose sole purpose is to educate the public on the sins of slavery, including the Old Slave Mart Museum in Charleston and the Lest We Forget Museum of Slavery in Philadelphia. In Montgomery, Alabama, the Equal Justice Initiative opened the first national memorial to the victims of lynchings in 2018.

Even so, these memorials to victims of racial violence will continue to face stiff competition from the many public efforts to honor the Confederacy. Just over 1,500 Confederate monuments populated the American landscape according to one estimate in 2016. This number is now slightly lower, largely because some cities removed their Confederate monuments in the aftermath of the white supremacist violence in Charleston and Charlottesville. But we must keep in mind the Confederacy's memory is enshrined not only in statues and stone markers. Eighty counties or cities are named after Confederates. Over one hundred public schools bear the names of Confederate icons such as Robert E. Lee, Stonewall Jackson, and Jefferson Davis. Six Southern states observe official holidays honoring the Confederacy or its leaders.[1] Trust me when I say that as a white, native Southerner, it's easy for people like me to grow up without giving much thought to those who endured the hardships and horrors of slavery, lynch mobs, and white supremacist terrorism.

Our memorials say a great deal about whose lives we are encouraged to remember. Consider this chapter a written memorial to the many victims of racial violence and torture whose lives and humanity we are all too often encouraged to forget.

Slavery

When we hear any public talk about slavery today, it's usually in reference to ISIS. The media goes to great lengths to detail ISIS's practice of slavery, particularly the sexual enslavement of Yazidi women and children. Of course, we should pay attention to these stories. Many innocent people are suffering a horrible fate at ISIS's hands. We should also take seriously how ISIS uses slavery not only to recruit but also to threaten the West. "We will conquer your Rome, break your crosses, and enslave your women," warned ISIS's spokesperson back in 2014. "If we do not reach that time, then our children and grandchildren will reach it, and they will sell your sons as slaves at the slave market."[2]

Most Muslim scholars find ISIS's choice to institute slavery abhorrent, noting the practice has been abolished throughout the Muslim world for over a century. The media doesn't pay a whole lot of attention to these refutations. This is because, as Kecia Ali puts it, slavery "fits into familiar narratives of Muslim barbarity."[3] Repudiating slavery does not.

Slavery has a long history in many parts of the world, from Europe to Africa to the Americas. People of many different cultural and religious groups are guilty of enslaving their fellow human beings. Muslims constitute one chapter of this history. White Euro-American Christians make up another. The transatlantic slave trade of European Christians holds a particular claim to infamy. It created a system of slavery rooted much more in claims of racial superiority than anything prior to it. In America, the "peculiar institution" took root in the South. Racialized violence and oppression became woven into the fabric of the United States as a result.

Between the sixteenth and nineteenth centuries, some thirty-five thousand voyages transported captured Africans, some of whom were Muslims, to Europe and the Americas to fill the need for agricultural and other manual labor. Over twelve million captives boarded ships during this time, though around two million perished on the journey. Most of the survivors ended up in the Caribbean or South America; only 5 percent landed in North America.[4] Congress abolished the slave trade in 1808, but the slave population kept multiplying. On the eve of the Civil War, some four million slaves lived in the United States, representing almost 13 percent of the population.[5]

The Constitutional Convention in 1787, in a compromise

that gave the South greater legislative and voting power, decreed slaves to be three-fifths of a person. Slaves were property, not fully human. Slaveholders held absolute property rights over slaves and punished them for a wide range of reasons, including disobedience, poor work performance, leaving the plantation without permission, violating the Sabbath, selling liquor, and learning to read and write.

Whipping was the most common form of corporal punishment, justified by reference to Jesus's own words: "And that servant, which knew his lord's will, and prepared not himself, neither did according to his will, shall be beaten with many stripes" (Luke 12:47).[6] Runaway slaves were branded on their palms, cheeks, shoulders, or buttocks to mark ownership and to help others identify them should they escape again. Execution awaited slaves who committed murder or participated in rebellions, but slaves presumed guilty of burglary, assault, or rape could be executed as well. Masters also raped and sexually assaulted slaves as a means to assert power over them.

The church offered ethical and theological justifications for slavery, though the Christian case for slavery took time to develop. Slaveholders initially feared they would be forced to free slaves who converted to Christianity. As colonies passed laws clarifying baptism did not equal emancipation, efforts to tie slavery to Christian teachings increased, as did the proselytizing of slaves.

Biblical arguments in defense of slavery were common by the nineteenth century. Proslavery Christians first and foremost appealed to the fact that the Old Testament describes patriarchs such as Abraham as slave owners. The laws governing the people of Israel assumed the practice. Another argument invoked the "Curse of Ham." According to Genesis, when Noah's son Ham saw his father naked and told his brothers, Noah cursed him and his son Canaan: "Cursed be Canaan; lowest of slaves shall he be to his brothers" (Genesis 9:25). The curse mattered for the slavery business because of the assumption Canaan was black and lived in Africa. His African descendants therefore shared in the curse.

Proslavery Christians also found ammunition in the New Testament. "Slaves, obey your earthly masters with fear and trembling" (Ephesians 6:5), exhorts one author. The authors of Colossians and 1 Peter made similar commands.[7] The apostle Paul urges Philemon, a runaway slave, to return to his master. Proslavery Christians had little difficulty making texts like these fit into their overall justification for slavery. As James Henley Thornwell, the South's leading theologian, put it, "the relation betwixt the slave and his master is not inconsistent with the word of God."[8]

None of these appeals to the Bible went unchallenged. Prominent abolitionists went out of their way to undercut proslavery arguments by presenting a more humane version of Christianity. Frederick Douglass, a former slave, described slaveholding Christianity as the greatest perversion, insisting there was "the widest possible difference" between true Christianity and "the corrupt, slaveholding, women-whipping, cradle-plundering, partial and hypocritical Christianity of this land."[9]

Slaves themselves took refuge in Christianity. They learned dangerous stories from the Bible, stories their masters didn't want them to know, stories of God's people liberated from the yoke of Pharaoh. They stole away at night to pray, worship, and sing outside the supervision of white Christians. This was an illegal but necessary act of defiance given that slaves were determined to view Christianity not as the cause of their enslavement but as the vehicle for their freedom. In dire circumstances, they revolted and gave their masters a taste of their own medicine.

Despite these resistance efforts, slavery prevailed because white Christians worked so hard to justify it. To resist slavery was to resist the will of God.

Lynchings and Jim Crow Violence

Slavery normalized the brutal treatment of African Americans. With the abolition of slavery, white Americans had to find new ways to reinforce the racial caste system. One way was through lynchings. White mobs lynched approximately 3,200 black men, mostly in the South, between 1880 and 1940.[10]

Lynchings were spectator events. Mobs performed lynchings for white consumers who needed reassurances of white superiority. Stories and photographs of lynchings conveyed the message of white power irrespective of whether blacks attended these "performances." Lynchings amounted to racial terrorism. Their purpose was to inspire fear among blacks and to torment them with thoughts of the horrible fate awaiting them should they step out of line.

The 1916 lynching of Jesse Washington illustrates the horror and spectacle of white mob violence against blacks.[11] Washington was a teenager who lived just outside of Waco, Texas, on the farm of George Fryer. Local authorities arrested Washington after Fryer's wife, Lucy, was found murdered. Washington confessed to the murder, though his guilt and the circumstances of his confession are a matter of debate.[12] He was put on trial, with thousands of people pouring into town to view what was rumored to be a certain lynching. After four minutes of deliberation, the jury returned a guilty verdict. A mob in the courtroom seized Washington, placed a chain around his neck, and hauled him to the lawn in front of city hall. Along the way, the crowd stripped him of his clothes and beat him brutally. It's difficult to read accounts of Washington and not think of the moments leading up to Jesus's crucifixion. As the theologian James Cone points out, the cross and the lynching tree are very much intertwined in African American history.[13]

Close to ten thousand people looked on as Washington was hung from a tree while his semiconscious body was raised and lowered repeatedly into a bonfire. The crowd mutilated Washington's body, cutting off his fingers and toes and castrating him. Some of these body parts became souvenirs for the locals. Washington eventually burned to death. A local photographer, with cooperation from the mayor's office, took photographs of the entire spectacle from a window in city hall.

The number of spectators who came to watch Washington's lynching exceeded what was typical, but the types of people who came to watch and participate were representative of many lynchings. The crowds in Waco were filled with white folks from all walks of life, from farmers to schoolchildren to the mayor and police chief. The lynching was also typical in that most who witnessed the spectacle were Christian. White Christians attending this or other lynchings found a way to fit such grotesque violence against black men into their moral frameworks. They received help from white churches, many of which either approved of lynchings or otherwise remained silent and thereby complicit.

Other horror stories of lynchings could have been included here. One of the reasons I have a particular interest in this one is because I lived in Waco for four years. I was a Presbyterian minister at a church whose minister one century earlier had spoken out against Washington's lynching. He was one of the few. This church was also located just down the street from where the lynching occurred. Yet I knew nothing about this sordid affair until long after I moved from Waco. I have since learned there have been a few efforts here and there to establish a memorial to the lynching, but to no avail. This is clearly not an event many Wacoans want to memorialize.

Lynchings became less frequent by the dawn of the Civil Rights era in the 1950s. However, the growing challenges to Jim Crow segregation sparked new waves of racial terrorism and murder to keep blacks in line. Emmett Till, a Chicago teenager visiting relatives in Mississippi in 1955, was beaten, shot in the head, and dumped in a river for allegedly "wolf-whistling" at Carolyn Bryant, a white woman. At the time, Bryant accused Till of other lewd behavior, but in 2017, she confessed that many of her accusations about him were false.[14] In 1963, the KKK set off dynamite at the 16th Street Baptist Church in Birmingham, Alabama, killing four black girls and injuring many other churchgoers. One year later, the KKK and local police officers abducted and murdered three civil rights workers in Mississippi, burying their bodies in a remote dam. It took over six weeks for authorities to find the three men. Beyond these stories were many others involving mob beatings, cross burnings, and murders.

White supremacists bore significant responsibility for this racial terrorism, but many white Christians were complicit as well. In his "Letter from a Birmingham Jail" (1963), Martin Luther King Jr. took white moderate Christians to task for their failure to support the Civil Rights movement.[15] While blacks struggled against blatant injustices, white Christians stood by and mouthed "pious irrelevancies and sanctimonious trivialities." While blacks asserted their full personhood in the face of discrimination and violence, white Christians responded that these were irrelevant social issues "with which the gospel has no real concern." It dawned on King that the KKK wasn't the biggest obstacle to civil rights. White moderate Christians were.

White supremacist violence did not end with the Civil Rights legislation of the mid-1960s. King himself was assassinated by a white supremacist in 1968. Almost fifty years later, white supremacy continues to inspire horrific violence, including in an African American church in Charleston in 2015, and on the streets of Charlottesville in 2017.

The ongoing plague of race-based violence has given rise to the Black Lives Matter movement. This movement arose after the acquittal in 2013 of George Zimmerman, the neighborhood watch volunteer in Florida who shot and killed an unarmed black teenager named Trayvon Martin. Stories of unarmed black men shot or otherwise killed by police officers grabbed headlines in the years that followed, from Michael Brown, an unarmed young man in Ferguson shot by a white police officer, to Eric Garner, who suffocated to death in a chokehold by NYPD officers, to Tamir Rice, a twelve-year-old boy in Cleveland shot by two police officers who mistook his toy gun for a real one.

Black Lives Matter has devoted attention to these and many other instances in which black lives are devalued by law enforcement. Their concerns are substantiated by research. According to data gathered by the *Washington Post*, unarmed black Americans are five times more likely than unarmed white Americans to be killed by a police officer.[16]

The police officers who shoot and kill unarmed black men are not white supremacists for the most part. Many suffer from implicit bias, or largely unconscious stereotypes and attitudes toward black Americans. They have been socialized to view black men as prone to violence and aggression and often respond accordingly. Implicit bias is still dangerous, precisely because of the lethal forms it takes and because of its historical ties to the dehumanizing treatment of people of color that dates back centuries.

White Americans may be tempted to dismiss centuries of violence toward blacks as an unfortunate footnote to history. This is wishful thinking. Racialized violence is far more integral to national identity than many care to admit. Slavery fueled the development of American industrialization and capitalism, paving the way for the United States to become a global economic superpower by the twentieth century.[17] Jim Crow segregation and violence perpetuated economic disparities and sustained white privilege. These racial disparities persist to this day in the education, employment, and housing sectors as well as in the criminal justice system. The economic and social fabric of modern America arose not in spite of white supremacist violence but because of it.

White supremacy has not gone away. Its influence in the highest echelons of government is easily observed. During the 2016 election cycle, the KKK and the white nationalist alt-right movement gave enthusiastic support to candidate Donald Trump. Trump did little to discourage this. If anything, he facilitated white supremacy's comeback by retweeting messages from its most ardent proponents, by selecting the white nationalist William Johnson as a delegate to the Republican primary in California, and by making the darling of the white nationalist movement, Steve Bannon, the White House chief strategist.[18]

When Trump assumed office, he continued to offer nods of support to white supremacists. In his remarks after the murder in August 2017 of an antiracism protestor by a white supremacist in Charlottesville, Trump assigned blame to "many sides." He also insisted that both sides consisted of "very fine people," a not-so-subtle endorsement of those who chanted racist and anti-Semitic slogans during the Charlottesville protest. Trump's language earned praise from former KKK leader David Duke, who thanked the president for his "honesty and courage to tell the truth."[19] The episode serves as a reminder that racism remains a formidable force in American politics.

Torture

Torture features prominently in many of the violent episodes I've discussed so far. That's because torture is very much a part of our past. It's also a part of our present. Even so, most of the audiences I speak to more readily associate modern-day torture with ISIS, not us.

There's good reason for this. We have plenty of evidence pointing to ISIS's heinous acts against prisoners and others who run afoul of the organization. When Obama gave his controversial prayer breakfast speech in 2015, he did so on the heels of the release of a video showing ISIS captors burning alive a Jordanian pilot. Survivors have also recalled harrowing accounts of lashings, electric shocks, and the *shabeh*, or hanging prisoners from their hands for days. Tragically, we also know rape is the most common form of torture used by ISIS against women.

ISIS is a brutal organization. But we would be wrong to assume ISIS has a monopoly on torture. The United Nations Convention against Torture defines torture as intentionally inflicting physical or mental suffering on others in order to punish or intimidate them or to elicit a confession from them. By this definition, it's evident torture has played a significant role in the modern histories of both Europe and the United States.

The best-known examples come from Nazi Germany, where millions of people fell victim to torture. Day-to-day torture in Nazi concentration camps revolved around punishment for infractions. The main punishment was whipping, but also common were forced standing and kneeling, the use of attack dogs, and in some cases, suspending prisoners, smashing teeth, and ripping out fingernails. Torture also extended beyond the camps into German-occupied territories during World War II. In France, Nazi torturers assailed their victims by pouring salt in their wounds, slicing them with razors, electrocuting their extremities or anus, crushing their genitalia, and asphyxiating them through submersion in cold water.

The French were not only victims of modern torture; they were perpetrators of it. Many of the methods described in Nazi Germany were employed in French colonies. From Vietnam to Madagascar, evidence points to

French authorities beating, electrocuting, or water torturing prisoners and political dissidents. The French institutionalized torture during the Algerian War (1954–1962). Paul Aussaresses, a military officer who masterminded the brutal regime of torture against the Algerian National Liberation Front, wrote in his 2001 memoir: "Only rarely were the prisoners we questioned during the night still alive the next morning."[20]

The British used torture to suppress rebellions against colonial rule. During the Mau Mau Uprising in Kenya (1952–1960), the British conducted mass arrests, targeting anyone remotely suspected of being connected to the revolt. Prisoners were taken to detention camps, where they endured horrible treatment. Beatings were common. Men were castrated with pliers. Women were raped, in some instances with glass bottles. Forced labor was imposed. Disease and hunger were rampant.[21] In 2013, the British government compensated over five thousand Kenyan victims of torture from the era of the Mau Mau Uprising. This settlement signaled the government's first official acknowledgment of these atrocities. Another forty-one thousand Kenyans filed suit against the government in 2014 on grounds of human rights abuses and torture during the uprisings.[22]

The United States relied increasingly on torture as its superpower status rose after World War II. Already in the 1950s, the US government was learning as much as it could about how communist interrogators used a method known as DDD—Debility, Dependency, and Dread—to break down prisoners. In 1965, both the CIA and Army Special Forces adapted DDD torture for the Phoenix Program. The program's purpose was to capture civilians during the Vietnam War believed to be sympathetic to the communist Vietcong. The program established interrogation centers where CIA interrogators, with the help of the South Vietnamese, tortured prisoners to uncover Vietcong connections. Many of those detained and tortured were innocent, but this did not spare them from a gruesome fate. An Army intelligence officer testified at a hearing before the US House Operations Subcommittee that no one survived an interrogation under his supervision during the eighteen months he served with the program. At the same hearing, the CIA officer who directed the program in the late 1960s testified that almost twenty-one thousand died under his tenure, though the final death toll reached perhaps as many as forty thousand.[23]

The US government found other outlets for torture in the service of foreign policy. The most infamous case of US-sponsored training in torture is the School of the Americas, located at Fort Benning, Georgia. Established in 1946 to strengthen ties between the United States and Latin America militaries, the school developed a long track record of instructing future military dictators and officers in interrogation techniques, torture methods, and psychological warfare. Graduates of the school bear responsibility for the torture of tens of thousands of people across Latin America. Congress voted to close the school in 1999 after training manuals detailing torture and other repressive measures were made public. The school closed and then reopened under a new name.[24] It remains open to this day.

The War on Terror provided new opportunities for the United States to torture prisoners and those suspected of committing or inciting terrorist acts. Evidence of torture first emerged in 2003, when Amnesty International published reports detailing human rights abuses by the US military in Iraqi prisons. One year later, photos emerged depicting all sorts of cruelties: a pyramid of naked bodies stacked on top of one another, a hooded prisoner with electric wires attached to outstretched arms, a terrified inmate coming face-to-face with a menacing attack dog, a subdued prisoner led on a leash as if he were a dog. Abu Ghraib was only one of many places where abuses occurred. Human rights organizations tracked and reported instances of torture from Guantanamo Bay to CIA black sites around the world.

When the US Senate Intelligence Committee released its report in 2014 on torture during the War on Terror, a fuller picture of US complicity with torture emerged.[25] The report detailed "enhanced interrogation techniques" used by the CIA on prisoners and detainees, including sleep and sensory deprivation, forced rectal feeding, ice water "baths," rape, mock executions, and waterboarding. The report also revealed the CIA misled high-ranking government officials on the methods used in interrogation and the value of the information extracted from torture.

"We did some things that were contrary to our values," Obama confessed.[26] But were they against our values? The torture he was referring to wasn't a momentary lapse of moral judgment by a rogue intelligence agency. Nor was it the case of a few bad apples in the military letting off steam during a long deployment. Torture was carefully planned out and executed during the War on Terror, just as it has been in other instances in our modern history.

What's tragic is that support for torture in America is widespread, even though many Americans are hesitant to label what the CIA did as torture. A *Washington Post* poll in 2014 revealed almost 60 percent of Americans believed the CIA's violent interrogation methods were justified. If you break down respondents by race and religion, white Christians were more likely to approve, with 66 percent of white Catholics, 69 percent of white evangelicals, and 75 percent of white mainline Protestants indicating violent CIA interrogation methods were justified.[27]

* * *

All of the evidence points toward a sobering truth. Torture is antithetical neither to Western values nor to the values of many white Christians; it's reflective of them. Slavery and lynchings also reflect values once deeply held by white Christian Americans. The persistence of anti-black racism and white supremacy suggests these values still linger. What's even more sobering is the fact that the unjust and brutal treatment of human beings described in this chapter is a defining feature not of the Middle Ages but of the modern histories and identities of Western nations. We are who we are today not in spite of this violence but because of it.

The time has come to memorialize this violence and to come to terms with it both publicly and politically. Only then can we make amends for our past crimes against humanity and pursue a future in which we are fully committed to the value and dignity of all human beings.

Notes

1. Southern Poverty Law Center, "Whose Heritage? Public Symbols of the Confederacy," 2016, 5, PDF, http://tinyurl.com/y9p8g2rg.

2. Graeme Wood, "What ISIS Really Wants," *The Atlantic*, March 2015, https://tinyurl.com/mb5os8d.

3. Kecia Ali, "The Truth about Islam and Sex Slavery History Is More Complicated Than You Think," *Huffington Post*, August 19, 2015, http://tinyurl.com/ybthg4j7.

4. Heather Andrea Williams, *American Slavery: A Very Short Introduction* (Oxford: Oxford University Press, 2014), 15–16.

5. "Census of 1860 Population-Effect on the Representation of the Free and Slave States," *New York Times*, April 5, 1860, http://tinyurl.com/y7rooh6u.

6. This citation comes from the King James Version of the Bible.

7. See Colossians 3:22, 1 Peter 2:18.

8. Mark A. Noll, "The Bible and Slavery," in *Religion and the American Civil War*, ed. Randall M. Miller, Harry S. Stout, and Charles Reagan Wilson (New York: Oxford University Press, 1998), 45.

9. Frederick Douglass, *Narrative of the Life of Frederick Douglass, an American Slave* (Boston: Anti-Slavery Office, 1845), 117.

10. Amy Louise Wood, *Lynching and Spectacle: Witnessing Racial Violence in America, 1890–1940* (Chapel Hill: University of North Carolina Press, 2009), 3.

11. For a discussion of Jesse Washington's lynching, see Wood, *Lynching and Spectacle*, 179–83.

12. Patricia Bernstein, *The First Waco Horror: The Lynching of Jesse Washington and the Rise of the NAACP* (College Station: Texas A&M University Press, 2006), 96; Julie Buckner Armstrong, *Mary Turner and the Memory of Lynching* (Athens: University of Georgia Press, 2011), 60.

13. James H. Cone, *The Cross and the Lynching Tree* (Maryknoll, NY: Orbis, 2011).

14. Richard Pérez-Peña, "Woman Linked to 1955 Emmett Till Murder Tells Historian Her Claims Were False," *New York Times*, January 27, 2017, http://tinyurl.com/yaamfnwn.

15. Martin Luther King Jr., "Letter from a Birmingham Jail," African Studies Center—University of Pennsylvania, April 16, 1963, http://tinyurl.com/y9xqb2xn.

16. Wesley Lowery, "Aren't More White People Than Black People Killed by Police? Yes, but No," *Washington Post*, July 11, 2016, http://tinyurl.com/y7nq7332.

17. Edward E. Baptist, *The Half Has Never Been Told: Slavery and the Making of American Capitalism* (New York: Basic Books, 2014); Sven Beckert, *Empire of Cotton: A Global History* (New York: Vintage, 2014); Greg Grandin, *The Empire of Necessity: Slavery, Freedom, and Deception in the New World* (New York: Metropolitan Books, 2014).

18. Mehdi Hasan, "The Numbers Don't Lie: White Far-Right Terrorists Pose a Clear Danger to Us All," *The Intercept*, May 31, 2017, http://tinyurl.com/y9e2m4kw.

19. Glenn Thrush and Maggie Haberman, "Trump Gives White Supremacists an Unequivocal Boost," *New York Times*, August 15, 2017, http://tinyurl.com/yd77heba.

20. Cited in Bruce Hoffman, *Inside Terrorism* (New York: Columbia University Press, 2006), 60.

21. Caroline Elkins, *Imperial Reckoning: The Untold Story of Britain's Gulag in Kenya* (New York: Henry Holt, 2005).

22. Katie Engelhart, "40,000 Kenyans Accuse UK of Abuse in Second Mau Mau Case," *The Guardian*, October 29, 2014, http://tinyurl.com/ycdyn499.

23. Michael Otterman, *American Torture: From the Cold War to Abu Ghraib and Beyond* (London: Pluto, 2007), 71; Seymour M. Hersh, "Moving Targets: Will the Counter-Insurgency Plan in Iraq Repeat the Mistakes of Vietnam?," *The New Yorker*, December 15, 2003, http://tinyurl.com/y6wtof3q.

24. Rebecca Gordon, *Mainstreaming Torture: Ethical Approaches in the Post-9/11 United States* (New York: Oxford University Press, 2014), 69, 132.

25. For the full report, see Senate Select Committee on Intelligence, *Committee Study of the Central Intelligence Agency's Detention and Interrogation Program*, December 3, 2014, http://tinyurl.com/hltk455.

26. "Press Conference by the President," The White House Office of the Press Secretary, August 1, 2014, http://tinyurl.com/yblddmg7.

27. Sarah Posner, "Christians More Supportive of Torture than Non-Religious Americans," *Religion Dispatches*, December 16, 2014, http://tinyurl.com/m3nybrf.

7

Who Lives, Who Dies, Who Tells Your Story

I don't remember much about elementary school academics. But I do remember the stories of settlers and soldiers fighting Native Americans from the unit on Alabama history in my fourth grade class. I developed an obsession with the battles that paved the way for courageous pioneers to create the great state of Alabama.

The most exciting one was the Battle of Horseshoe Bend (1814), where the military general and future president Andrew Jackson defeated the Creek tribe that had fought hard to prevent the United States from expanding into its territory. I remember making a clay model of the Creek fort Jackson's army ultimately destroyed as a way to bring the battle to life. I was able to visualize Jackson and his troops overpowering this fortified village tucked away in a horseshoe-shaped bend in the Tallapoosa River. Jackson was my hero.

What I don't remember was learning anything about what happened after the battle. I didn't learn Jackson's troops cut off the tips of the noses of Creek corpses to conduct a body count, or that soldiers made bridle reins from the skin of the same corpses. Jackson was defending the nation from a savage threat, I learned. Neither he nor other white Americans were the source of savagery.

Something else I didn't learn in fourth grade or any grade was that Jackson's battle against the Creeks was part of a larger genocidal project dating back to Columbus. Words like "genocide" were not a part of the vocabulary Alabama school children encountered when learning about Native Americans. My hunch is that many schoolchildren today still don't have textbooks that describe what happened to Native Americans as genocide.

It really wasn't until I went to graduate school to become a religious historian that I came to appreciate just how subjective history is. History is not simply about what happened. History is a story, told from a certain perspective with a certain purpose. When historians are doing their job, they push beyond "just the facts" to uncover this perspective and purpose. Historians want to know the answers to questions like: Who gets to tell the story of what happened? From what viewpoint? Who or what is included in the story? Who or what is left out? For what purpose?

The story of Native Americans I learned in fourth grade

was told from the perspective of white Americans trying to justify the violence and bloodshed that made US expansion possible. It certainly was not told from the perspective of or with any empathy for Native Americans. The same holds true for other atrocities that appear in Western history, including the Holocaust and the dropping of the atomic bombs on Japan to end World War II. These stories are often narrated in a way that either favors the perspectives of the victors or otherwise leaves out inconvenient details that would cast an unflattering light on Western and Christian perpetrators of mass atrocities.

It's time to take another look at these monumental episodes in Western history and to adopt a different perspective, one that takes more seriously both the sufferings of the "losers" and the moral failings of the "winners."

Genocide

In 2016, US Secretary of State John Kerry declared that ISIS was guilty of genocide against Yazidis, Christians, and Shi'a Muslims in Iraq and Syria. His statement came after the House of Representatives unanimously passed a resolution classifying ISIS's atrocities against Christians and other religious and ethnic minorities as genocide. Accounts of Christian suffering, more so than the suffering of Muslims and other religious and ethnic minorities, prompted the resolution. These accounts were of particular concern to politicians with a conservative Christian base worried about the threats posed to the West by "radical Islam." This serves as a reminder that what constitutes genocide, not to mention who is a perpetrator or victim of it, is always driven by political factors.

We know this lesson all too well from Western history. Both the United States and Europe have wrestled with horrific episodes of genocide. At the same time, larger political forces have dictated how we remember these episodes, including whether we are to view them as genocide or as necessary and even heroic events in the unfolding of our national destinies.

The most disastrous manifestation of genocide in American history is the extermination of the continent's indigenous peoples. When the Italian explorer Christopher Columbus "sailed the ocean blue" in 1492 on behalf of the Spanish Crown, he ended up not at his intended destination, Japan, but in the Caribbean. His fateful encounter with the indigenous peoples of the island he renamed "Hispaniola" was followed by widespread disease, destruction, and death. By the numbers, the death toll was staggering. Most of the eight million people living on the island died or were killed off in the course of two decades after Columbus landed.[1] When we widen the geographical and chronological scope, the lethal impact of European contact is even more astounding. In 1492, an estimated sixteen million indigenous people lived in the continental United States. By 1900, only 237,000 native peoples were left, though their numbers recovered a little over the course of the twentieth century. Even so, that's a depopulation rate of 98.4 percent in the span of four centuries.[2]

The introduction of European diseases played a huge part in this rapid decline. This perhaps gives the impression most native peoples died inadvertently from European contact. Not so. Disease and intentional extermination went hand in hand.[3] European attitudes toward indigenous peoples, characterized by an utter disregard for their humanity, fueled the aggressive treatment of these populations and facilitated the spread of disease. This left them more vulnerable to attack and less capable of holding off the aggressive expansion of European colonizers.

Deliberate efforts to purge the continent of indigenous peoples contributed to their decline. In the Pequot War (1636–1637), Puritans settlers targeted hundreds of defenseless natives by setting wigwams on fire and burning alive their inhabitants, mostly women, children, and the elderly. In the Sand Creek Massacre (1864), a US cavalry destroyed a Cheyenne and Arapaho village in Colorado, killing or maiming as many people as they could find, most of them women and children. They did this at the command of Colonel John Chivington, who ordered his troops to "kill and scalp all, little and big."[4]

One of the swiftest genocides of a particular tribe involved the Yuki of northern California. With the onset of the California Gold Rush in 1848, white settlers entered the territory and proceeded to hunt down and slaughter indigenous peoples, irrespective of sex or age. Much of this was done with implicit state support. By 1880, the Yuki population, numbering 20,000 just three decades before, had fallen to 168.[5] The Yuki were not the only ones to experience such decimation. California's overall indigenous population dropped from 150,000 to 30,000 between 1846 and 1870.[6] Disease, forced labor, and confinement on reservations all contributed to the death toll, but so did murders and massacres.

While the UN defines genocide as the intentional effort to kill off a population, genocide is not only that. It also involves actions, even unintentional ones, that destroy the spirit or soul of a people by undermining or obliterating the values and cultural norms that give their community meaning and life. Scholars call this *cultural genocide*.[7] Cultural genocide became part of US policy with the Civilization Fund Act of 1819. The act provided funds to benevolent societies to help educate and "civilize" Native Americans according to white, Christian standards. Much of this was done through Christian missionary schools. These schools did not see their work as what we would call "genocide" today, but without a doubt, they worked hard to impose their understanding of racial and religious superiority on indigenous children in the hopes of assimilating them to non–Native American cultural norms.

The Indian Removal Act of 1830 also contributed to cultural genocide. The act instituted the compulsory relocation of indigenous peoples from the South to federal lands west of the Mississippi River. The most significant instance of this was the Trail of Tears, a series of forced relocations in the

1830s that led to thousands of Native Americans dying en route due to starvation and disease. Those who survived the brutal journey found themselves in barren reservations, disconnected from ancestral lands and confined to an existence at odds with cultural and spiritual customs.

The ideological underpinnings of Native American genocide came from the racial and religious theory known as Manifest Destiny. Manifest Destiny dictated that white Christians had a right if not a divine obligation to take control of Native American lands and to expand their dominion over the continent.

The phrase was first coined in the mid-nineteenth century, but the core idea existed already in colonial times. English Puritans often told this story in biblical terms, casting themselves as the new Israel, inheritors of a new Promised Land. The Puritans assigned Native Americans the role of Amalekites. In the biblical account, God commands Israel's leader, King Saul, to wipe out the Amalekites. In 1675, while at war against the Narragansett tribe, Captain Samuel Appleton prayed that "our Israel" would prevail "over this cursed Amalek." He was convinced God desired perpetual war against these heathens "until he have destroyed them." A decade later, the Reverend Cotton Mather called for vengeance "against the Amalek that is now annoying this Israel in the Wilderness" that would last "until they are consumed."[8]

These views persisted under the more fully developed doctrine of Manifest Destiny in the nineteenth century, minus the Amalekite references. Caleb Cushing, a prominent politician and supporter of Manifest Destiny, told the Massachusetts State Legislature in 1859: "We belong to that excellent white race." It's the task of whites, he went on to say, "to Christianize and civilize, to command and to be obeyed, to conquer and to reign." Cushing saw other whites as equals, but insisted "I do not admit as my equals the red men of America."[9]

Another prominent politician of that era, Senator Thomas Hart Benton of Missouri, was adamant "the White race alone received the divine command, to subdue and replenish the earth."[10] A newspaper in California summed up the racist and religious impulses behind the genocidal doctrine in 1865, stating that if necessary, "let there be a crusade" against native peoples and let "every man that can carry and shoot a gun turn out and hunt the red devils to their holes and bury them."[11]

It's unfortunate we struggle so much to acknowledge the history of genocide in North America. An uproar occurred in 2012 when the College Board determined that high school students preparing for the Advanced Placement (AP) US history exam should be familiar with the genocide of indigenous peoples. Two years later, the Republican National Committee (RNC) passed a resolution requesting a congressional inquiry into the AP US history framework. The RNC expressed deep concern that the framework "presents a biased and inaccurate view of many important events in American history, including the motivations and actions of the

17th–19th century settlers."[12] Translation: don't use the word "genocide," and for heaven's sake, don't even think about mentioning white Christians as perpetrators of genocide. Instead, let's see these white colonists and settlers as courageous explorers committed to the spread of freedom and democracy. Fear and anxiety about facing our violent past drives these and other efforts to sanitize textbooks and curricula of any mention of Native American genocide.

While many Americans hesitate to think of genocide as part of their history, they have no such hang-ups about attributing intentional mass murder to European history. The Holocaust in Nazi Germany represents the one instance of genocide that garners significant acknowledgement in history books and political spaces on both sides of the Atlantic. The Holocaust refers to the systemic persecution and murder of six million Jews from 1933 to 1945.[13] The Nazis tortured or executed millions more people during this time as well, including Russians, Poles, Roma, communists, socialists, the physically and mentally disabled, and LGBTQ persons.

Within a few years of Hitler's rise to power, Germany transformed anti-Semitic racial theories into laws prohibiting Jews from citizenship and from engaging in sexual relations with people of pure German stock. Anti-Jewish discrimination increasingly turned violent. In November 1938, at the instigation of the Nazi party, rioters destroyed hundreds of Jewish shops and synagogues and killed close to a hundred Jews in a wave of pogroms known as *Kristallnacht*. Police arrested thirty thousand Jewish men, sending many of them to concentration camps.[14] By the outbreak of World War II in 1939, millions of Jews found themselves under Nazi control. In the next six years, the Final Solution was in full force as Jews were deported, incarcerated, starved, tortured, and exterminated in mass numbers.

Much of the genocidal violence against Jews is well known. Gas chambers became the most prominent vehicles for mass extermination. After German soldiers developed psychological fatigue from shooting large numbers of civilians at close range, gas chambers became a means of helping the soldiers cope better with the anguish by physically distancing them from the killing. At the height of Jewish deportations, close to six thousand Jews per day were gassed in Auschwitz.[15] Concentration camps were also the sites of beatings, forced labor, starvation, widespread disease, and brutal medical experiments.

The Nazi program of genocide was the culmination of centuries of Jew-hatred throughout Europe. Medieval Christian treatment of Jews set the stage for a history of atrocities. Christians accused Jews of desecrating the eucharistic host or bread, poisoning wells during the Black Death, and murdering Christian children to use their blood in making matzoth for Passover. Jews also experienced expulsions across Europe throughout the Middle Ages.

The Reformation did not make things better for Jews. In his treatise "On the Jews and Their Lies" (1543), Martin Luther encouraged Christians to burn down synagogues, destroy Jewish homes, confiscate Jewish prayer books and writings, and prohibit rabbis from teaching on pain of death.[16] Four hundred years later, Luther's treatise found a new audience in the Nazis. They proudly displayed it during annual Nazi political rallies in Nuremberg and saw Luther as a visionary when it came to the threat posed by Jews to Germany.

This history of Christian hatred for Jews paved the way for German Christian support of the Nazi Party. Hitler campaigned for a return to traditional values and against communism, prostitution, and same-sex relations. His promises resonated with Protestant leaders. They saw in Hitler someone who would restore the church's social and political privilege and prestige. These factors, more so than anti-Semitism, drove much of the initial Christian support for Hitler.[17] But anti-Semitism was widespread among Christians, even if many were less explicit about it than their new *Führer*.

The Protestant movement that gave the greatest support to the Nazis and its anti-Semitic ideology was the German Christians (*Deutsche Christen*). The German Christians believed Jewishness was a racial category. They sought a purer people's church (*Volkskirche*) in which pastors and parishioners with Jewish ancestry were marginalized or barred. They wanted to remove any trace of Jewishness from Protestantism, rejecting the authority of the Old Testament and the Jewish background of Jesus. German Christians held considerable power, occupying key positions in national church governing bodies, as bishops, in theological faculties, and on local church councils.

Christian resistance did materialize. A movement known as the Confessing Church (*Bekennende Kirche*) pushed back against some Nazi excesses. It took particular aim at the Aryan Paragraph, a clause that sought to remove Christian clergy with Jewish ancestry from church offices. This countermovement gave rise to heroic figures such as the Lutheran pastors Martin Niemöller and Dietrich Bonhoeffer. Both ended up as prisoners in concentration camps as a result of their subversive activities. Bonhoeffer tragically was executed just two weeks before the Americans liberated his camp in 1945.

But heroes were few and far between. The Confessing Church showed far more concern for Christians of Jewish ancestry than Jews themselves. In the now famous Barmen Declaration (1934), the Confessing Church took the German Christians to task for their heresy. Yet the declaration made no mention of Jews and no effort to dismantle the underlying anti-Semitism of the Nazi state.[18]

The Catholic Church was more skeptical of Hitler's rise to power. With Pope Pius XI, there was even a bold attempt to call out the Nazi state. In the encyclical *On the Church and the German Reich* (1937), the pope condemned neo-paganism, idolizing the state, and "the so-called myth of race and blood."[19] The pope died two years later. His successor, Pius XII, was far more hesitant to clash with Germany. In 1942, he gave a much-anticipated Christmas radio address. By this time, he had detailed information on the suffering and killing of Jews. Urged by Britain and the United States to condemn these crimes in his broadcast, Pius avoided any explicit reference to Jews. He kept his remarks vague, expressing sorrow for injustices carried out during the war.[20]

Neither Catholics nor Protestants, from the pulpits or the pews, generated significant resistance to the Nazis and their persecution of Jews. Most Christians were silent in the face of these injustices, even as awareness of what was taking place had spread widely by the early 1940s. After the war, Christians had to take a serious look at how they failed victims of the Holocaust. It was in this time that Niemöller made his now famous remarks about Christian inaction:

First they came for the Socialists, and I did not speak out—
Because I was not a Socialist.

Then they came for the Trade Unionists, and I did not speak out—
Because I was not a Trade Unionist.

Then they came for the Jews, and I did not speak out—
Because I was not a Jew.

Then they came for me—and there was no one left to speak for me.[21]

Niemöller recognized the failure to actively speak out and challenge the persecution and extermination of Jews amounted to complicity in the Holocaust.

The Holocaust was neither the first nor last genocidal event in twentieth-century Europe. More could be said of the mass killing of over one million Armenians by the Ottoman Empire during World War I,[22] or the twenty-six thousand Bosnian Muslim civilians killed or massacred during the

Bosnian War (1992–1995) and the many more who disappeared, became displaced, or were raped.[23] All of these events remind us that genocidal instincts and their catastrophic consequences are not limited to ISIS.

Atomic Annihilation

An undeniable threat to global security is the desire of some terrorist organizations or rogue states to develop or acquire nuclear weapons. Western governments have sometimes overhyped these threats. The most infamous example is the Bush administration's false claim in 2002 and 2003 that Iraq's Saddam Hussein was developing weapons of mass destruction that included nuclear weapons. Even so, concerns about terrorist organizations such as al-Qaeda and ISIS attempting to add nuclear weapons to their deadly arsenal are well founded.

If history is our guide, however, we shouldn't assume nuclear weapons are automatically safe and secure in our hands. The only instances of nuclear weapons being used to kill mass numbers of civilians come neither from rogue states such as North Korea or Iran, nor from Muslim terrorist organizations. They come from the US attack on Japan at the end of World War II. On August 6, 1945, an American warplane dropped an atomic bomb on Hiroshima. Three days later, another bomb was dropped on Nagasaki.

US political orthodoxy dictates the atomic bombs prompted the Japanese to surrender and prevented at least half a million American casualties that otherwise would have occurred during an invasion of Japan. President Harry S.

Truman is responsible for this now-entrenched narrative. In a radio address that took place on the same day as the Nagasaki bombing, Truman justified the atomic bombings by insisting: "We have used it in order to shorten the agony of war, in order to save the lives of thousands and thousands of young Americans."[24]

What is less known is most five-star generals and admirals opposed Truman's decision to use the bomb. World War II military heroes, from Douglas MacArthur to Dwight D. Eisenhower, thought Truman was wrong. They insisted the Japanese were all but defeated and were likely to surrender without an American invasion. Some military leaders also articulated strong moral objections. Admiral William Leahy called the atomic bomb a "barbarous weapon" that reflected "an ethical standard common to the barbarians of the Dark Ages."[25] He considered the targeting of large numbers of civilians, including women and children, a violation of the laws of war and of the Christian faith.

But public opinion was in favor of the bombings, in part because anti-Japanese racism was so rampant. Truman himself held deeply racist views toward the Japanese, describing them in his diary as "savages" who were "ruthless, merciless, and fanatic."[26] After the attack on Pearl Harbor in 1941, growing concerns that Japanese Americans were a "fifth column" bent on destroying the country from within placed pressure on Truman's predecessor, President Franklin D. Roosevelt, to respond to this presumed threat. In 1942, Roosevelt issued a proclamation that paved the way for the forced relocation of over 120,000 Japanese Americans to internment camps.[27]

Conservative estimates put the death toll from the bombings at close to 250,000, with civilians making up the overwhelming majority of victims.[28] Some of the deaths came from immediate vaporization, while others died from incineration or from the "black rain" that spread radioactive material after the bombings. This gruesome aftermath did not make the Truman administration waver from the story that the atomic annihilation of large civilian populations served a greater good.

To this day, efforts to show remorse or to raise critical questions about the bombings are met with fierce opposition. In 1995, a Smithsonian exhibit featuring fuselage from the Enola Gay, the B-29 plane that dropped the first atomic bomb, came under fire for incorporating analyses of topics that challenged the dominant narrative, including the morality of dropping the bomb, the death toll in Hiroshima, and the number of American casualties avoided because of Truman's decision to use the bomb. Congressional members and some veterans groups succeeded in having the exhibition scaled down to exclude any information or context that challenged the orthodox narrative.[29]

In 2016, Obama became the first sitting US president to visit Hiroshima. He gave a speech at the Hiroshima Peace Memorial Museum commemorating the lives lost and expressing hope for a future in which Hiroshima and Nagasaki are known not as the beginning of atomic warfare but as the catalyst for a "moral awakening."[30] While Obama did not apologize for the bombings, critics still pounced on his decision to visit Hiroshima. Donald Trump, the Republican presidential frontrunner at the time, attacked Obama for focusing more on the victims of Hiroshima than Pearl Harbor. Former Republican vice-presidential nominee Sarah Palin called his trip an "apology lap" and accused him of "dissing our vets."[31]

Trump's presidency has not inaugurated a new era of soul-searching about the morality of targeting mass numbers of civilians for nuclear annihilation. If anything, his tenure in office marks the most significant threat of a Hiroshima repeat. Throughout the presidential campaign, Trump insisted nuclear weapons should remain on the table. When pressed on this point by MSNBC host Chris Matthews, Trump asked rhetorically: "Somebody hits us within ISIS—you wouldn't fight back with a nuke?"[32] What was frightening was that people across the political spectrum took Trump at his word, a fear that only intensified after he took office.

★ ★ ★

Every category of unjust violence attributed to Muslim extremists can be found in Western history. In some cases, the perpetrators understood, articulated, or justified their actions within a Christian framework. In other cases, Christians gave implicit support to unjust violence or otherwise found ways to fit this violence into their moral scaffolding. In still other cases, the culprits were not Christian but were nonetheless acting on behalf of US or European governments.

Given this track record, why haven't those of us in the majority population engaged in the amount of soul-searching we've asked of our Muslim neighbors? To answer this question, we have to know something about how Islamophobia works.

"Know the function, the very serious function of racism, which is distraction," argues the noted author Toni Morrison.[33] Racism distracts African Americans by forcing them to explain themselves and their existence to a white population that never seems fully convinced.

This observation holds for anti-Muslim racism as well, including assumptions that Muslims are presumed guilty of supporting terrorism until they convince us otherwise. Relentlessly asking Muslims to condemn terrorism is a distraction. It forces Muslims to explain themselves, to prove their innocence, to defend their humanity. Yet the rest of us never seem satisfied with their efforts. So we keep asking the same question. Over and over.

But asking Muslims to condemn terrorism distracts the rest of us too. It keeps us from facing our own violent history and from understanding how Western nations rose to power and prominence on waves of unjust violence. It keeps us from asking critical questions about how our current foreign policies or national security initiatives contribute to a violent world order. It keeps us from applying the word "terrorist" to violent people who look like me, share my religious or cultural background, or serve in my government.

When we are this distracted, we become blind to the hypocrisy involved in asking Muslims to reject the kinds of violence we would never be asked to reject. I for one have never been asked to denounce the Holocaust, to repudiate slavery, or to apologize for the atomic annihilation of Japanese civilians. When Wade Michael Page murdered six Sikhs in cold blood at a gurdwara outside of Milwaukee, or when Anders Behring Breivik massacred seventy-seven people in Norway, no one asked me to condemn white supremacist violence. I don't have to explain myself, defend my Christian background, or prove my innocence over and over again in the court of public opinion. I am presumed innocent. I am afforded a privilege my Muslim neighbors are not.

It's time to end the distractions and to spend more energy on coming to terms with unjust Western violence. Doing so won't kill us. Nor will it hamper us in the fight against terrorism. What it will do is make us more honest in our assessments of the causes and consequences of unjust violence. It will keep in check the feelings of cultural and religious superiority that drive false narratives of barbarous Muslims versus civilized Westerners. And it will open the door to asking better questions of our Muslim neighbors, questions that presume the best of them and not the worst.

Notes

1. David E. Stannard, *American Holocaust: Columbus and the Conquest of the New World* (New York: Oxford University Press, 1992), x.

2. Chris Mato Nunpa, "A Sweet-Smelling Sacrifice: Genocide, the Bible, and the Indigenous Peoples of the United States, Selected Examples," in *Confronting Genocide: Judaism, Christianity, Islam*, ed. Steven Leonard Jacobs (Lanham, MD: Lexington, 2009), 61.

3. Stannard, *American Holocaust*, xii.

4. Adam Jones, *Genocide: A Comprehensive Introduction* (New York: Routledge, 2006), 73.

5. Jones, *Genocide*, 73–75.

6. Benjamin Madley, *An American Genocide: The United States and the California Indian Catastrophe, 1846–1873* (New Haven: Yale University Press, 2016), 3.

7. George E. Tinker, *Missionary Conquest: The Gospel and Native American Cultural Genocide* (Minneapolis: Fortress Press, 1993).

8. John Corrigan, "New Israel, New Amalek: Biblical Exhortations to Religious Violence," in *From Jeremiad to Jihad: Religion, Violence, and America*, ed. John D. Carlson and Jonathan H. Ebel (Berkeley: University of California Press, 2012), 114.

9. Brendan C. Lindsay, *Murder State: California's Native American Genocide, 1846–1873* (Lincoln: University of Nebraska Press, 2012), 55.

10. Nunpa, "Sweet-Smelling Sacrifice," 56.

11. Lindsay, *Murder State*, 67.

12. Cited in Tanya H. Lee, "The Native American Genocide and the Teaching of US History," *Truthout*, April 1, 2015, http://tinyurl.com/y96sofnu.

13. Data on the death toll of the Holocaust comes from the United States Holocaust Memorial Museum. The museum's estimates derive from wartime reports produced by individuals who implemented Nazi policy, along with postwar demographic studies on population decline. See United States Holocaust Memorial Museum, "Documenting Numbers of Victims of the Holocaust and Nazi

Persecution," Holocaust Encyclopedia, http://tinyurl.com/y7mlawnk.

14. Jones, *Genocide*, 150.

15. United States Holocaust Memorial Museum, "Gassing Operations," Holocaust Encyclopedia, http://tinyurl.com/yb4236gt.

16. Martin Luther, "Concerning the Jews and Their Lies," in *The Protestant Reformation*, ed. Hans J. Hillerbrand (New York: Harper Perennial, 2009), 137–49.

17. Robert P. Ericksen, *Complicity in the Holocaust: Churches and Universities in Nazi Germany* (Cambridge: Cambridge University Press, 2012), 37.

18. "The Theological Declaration of Barmen," in *The Constitution of the Presbyterian Church (U.S.A.): Part I, Book of Confessions* (Louisville: Office of the General Assembly, 2014), 285–97.

19. Pope Pius XI, *Mit Brennender Sorge*, March 14, 1937, http://tinyurl.com/y7ajpouk.

20. Ericksen, *Complicity in the Holocaust*, 130.

21. Cited in United States Holocaust Memorial Museum, "Martin Niemöller: 'First They Came for the Socialists . . . ,'" Holocaust Encyclopedia, http://tinyurl.com/ybq2qx8u.

22. Neil Faulkner, *Lawrence of Arabia's War: The Arabs, The British and the Remaking of the Middle East in WWI* (New Haven: Yale University Press, 2016), 78.

23. Jacqueline Ching, *Genocide and the Bosnian War* (New York: Rosen, 2009).

24. Harry S. Truman, "Radio Report to the American People on the Potsdam Conference," Public Papers: Harry S. Truman, 1945–1953, Harry S. Truman Presidential Library and Museum, August 9, 1945, http://tinyurl.com/yd4xku8s.

25. Phillips Payson O'Brien, *How the War Was Won: Air-Sea Power and Allied Victory in World War II* (Cambridge: Cambridge University Press, 2015), 477.

26. Wilson D. Miscamble, *The Most Controversial Decision: Truman, the Atomic Bomb, and the Defeat of Japan* (Cambridge: Cambridge University Press, 2011), 70.

27. Joshua Chambers-Letson, "Imprisonment/Internment/Detention,"

in *The Routledge Companion to Asian American and Pacific Islander Literature*, ed. Rachel C. Lee (New York: Routledge, 2014), 148.

28. John W. Dower, *Cultures of War: Pearl Harbor/Hiroshima/9-11/Iraq* (New York: W. W. Norton, 2010), 199.

29. Karen de Witt, "Smithsonian Scales Back Exhibit of B-29 in Atomic Bomb Attack," *New York Times*, January 31, 1995, http://tinyurl.com/yb89f7m7.

30. "Text of President Obama's Speech in Hiroshima, Japan," *New York Times*, May 27, 2016, http://tinyurl.com/y7rrldez.

31. Phillip Rucker, "Sarah Palin Assails Obama for Hiroshima Visit," *Washington Post*, May 27, 2016, http://tinyurl.com/ycrbxx8d.

32. Robert Windrem and William M. Arkin, "What Does Donald Trump Really Think about Using Nuclear Weapons?," NBC News, September 28, 2016, http://tinyurl.com/ya49um8k.

33. Cited in T. Elon Dancy II, "The Black Male Body and the (Post?)Colonial University: Identity Politics and the Tyranny of Meritocracy," in *Black Men in the Academy: Narratives of Resiliency, Achievement, and Success*, ed. Brian L. McGowan, Robert T. Palmer, J. Luke Wood, and David F. Hibbler Jr. (Hampshire: Palgrave Macmillan, 2016), 165.

Conclusion: Assuming the Best of Our Muslim Neighbors

Just two miles from the Gettysburg Battlefield, the site of one of the most significant battles in the American Civil War, another battle erupted in the spring of 2017 on the campus of Gettysburg College. The student chapter of the Young Americans for Freedom (YAF) had invited the anti-Muslim hate speaker Robert Spencer to deliver a talk on campus on the dangers of Islamic fundamentalism.

Spencer was known for writing offensive and hostile books on Islam, including *The Truth about Muhammad: Founder of the World's Most Intolerant Religion* and *The Complete Infidel's Guide to the Koran*. His antics earned him a preeminent spot on the Southern Poverty Law Center's anti-Muslim extremist list. In 2013, Britain's home secretary, later prime minister, Theresa May, banned Spencer from entering the UK due to his record of hate speech. Spencer also had a track record of attracting some unsavory followers. Anders Behring Breivik, who murdered seventy-seven people in Norway in July 2011, cited Spencer's views on Islam 162 times in his online manifesto as justification for his own hatred of Muslims and immigrants.

Concerned students, staff, and faculty raised alarm bells. Spencer, they noted, promoted beliefs about Muslims antithetical to the college's mission of affirming the dignity and worth of all people. Providing Spencer with a platform for hate speech signaled to Muslims in the community that the college was willing to negotiate their dignity. YAF countered that Spencer represented much-needed diversity on the topic of Islam and that the college should uphold its commitments to freedom of speech at all costs.

College administrators, including the president, listened carefully to both sides, but in the end, they greenlighted the invitation on the grounds of freedom of speech. In an effort to provide an alternative perspective in anticipation of Spencer's visit, Gettysburg's Religious Studies Department and Peace and Justice Studies Program invited me to campus to give a public lecture on "professional Islamophobia"—the manufacturing of anti-Muslim hatred for professional and financial gain. Included in the lecture was a critique of Spencer's infamous career as a maligner of Muslims and the money he's received in doing it.

What's memorable about my time at Gettysburg, beyond the extraordinary hospitality I experienced from the college community, was what happened after my lecture. For the first time in my career, I received a security escort back to my hotel. The escort was no doubt prompted by the intensity of the campus debates surrounding Spencer's visit and some of the media attention the controversy was receiving. It was also perhaps a safety measure adopted in light of other controversies on college campuses earlier in the year that turned violent.

I've delivered plenty of public lectures where security or police officers were present. But I've never had to ride back to my hotel with a security escort. This seemed like a real low point in my career, even if the precautions were necessary. It spoke volumes about the enormous difficulties of engaging in a calm, measured conversation about Islam in the public arena. It also pointed to the real power people like Spencer have acquired to disrupt communities and to stir up tensions and hostilities toward Muslims and their allies.

We are at a crossroads when it comes to how we engage with our Muslim neighbors. We can continue to allow the likes of Spencer to dictate the terms of how we discuss Muslims on our campuses and in our communities. This inevitably means we will remain stuck in a defensive posture, expending our time and energy trying to prove whether or not Muslims are prone to violence and terrorism. Or we can reject this poisonous mindset and embrace a new paradigm, one that recalibrates our attitudes and fosters positive curiosity and respect toward Muslim communities.

Krister Stendahl, who was a New Testament scholar, a dean at Harvard Divinity School, and a Lutheran bishop in the Church of Sweden, developed such a paradigm. His paradigm contains three rules of interfaith understanding that hold much promise for fostering healthy relationships with people from religious traditions different than our own. First, let people of other religions define themselves. Don't allow their enemies to do it for them. Second, compare like with like. Don't compare the positive qualities of our religion with the negative qualities in other religions. Finally, develop "holy envy." Find that which is beautiful and moving within the religion of the other.

I will adopt and adapt Stendahl's three rules for interfaith understanding as a framework for engaging Muslim communities. I have used Stendahl's three rules in my public scholarship and even in my work at the State Department. Many of the audiences I work with, religious and secular, find them quite helpful. They offer a great first step for those who want to cultivate genuine friendships and relationships with Muslims but don't know how to start. They promote an understanding of Muslims that assumes the best of them.

These rules are more difficult to follow than they appear. That's because they will not work unless we allow Muslims to become our teachers and our windows into the world of Islam. The political and media establishments have taught us to view Muslims as objects of suspicion, not as sources of wisdom or insight. This means many of us harbor implicit biases against Muslims. These biases will not disappear easily, or without effort. But the more we allow these rules to guide us when reaching out to Muslim communities, the more progress we will make in building interfaith bridges that will endure the test of time.

Let People of Other Religions Define Themselves

The first rule is always to allow people of other religious traditions to define what their religion means to them. I often paraphrase the rule this way: learn from a religion's practitioners, not from its enemies.

It's easy to take for granted our ability to define what our own religion means to us when we are in the majority. I grew up a Presbyterian and served as a Presbyterian minister. Not once did I ever have to worry about an anti-Presbyterian network co-opting the Presbyterian narrative for nefarious purposes or attempting to define my Presbyterian faith for me. I imagine this is true for most Christians living in the West.

Not so for Muslims. The professional Islamophobia network doesn't want Muslims to tell their own stories. People like Robert Spencer, Pamela Geller, and Frank Gaffney go out of their way to be seen as Islam experts and to wrest control of Islam's narrative from Muslims. There's too much at stake for them financially and politically to allow Muslim Americans (or Muslims anywhere) to define themselves.

I mentioned in chapter 4 how the conspiracy theories promulgated by this network about a Muslim Brotherhood infiltration into the highest levels of the US government have gained traction in Washington. But I have also witnessed the network's growing influence amongst the general population. It's not uncommon for someone to attend one of my public lectures and either invoke stereotypes or employ tactics popularized by this industry. In some instances, this takes the form of some guy (it's almost always a guy) standing up during the Q&A to try to discredit everything I've just said about Islamophobia. The man in question opens up the Qur'an (which conveniently he has brought with him) and quotes aloud the so-called "sword verse" as proof of Islam's violence: "Wherever you encounter idolaters, kill them" (Q. 9:5). He then closes the Qur'an and, with a smug smile, tells everyone there's no such thing as Islamophobia, that Muslims follow an intolerant, hateful religion that requires them to persecute and murder infidels. How does he know? He's read their book! And within its pages, he's found the incriminating evidence. In his mind, this makes him an expert. It's the kind of reasoning and argumentation that comes right out of the professional Islamophobia network's playbook.

I used to lose my patience when stuff like this happened, complete with a not-so-subtle eye roll upon hearing some random guy quote the Qur'an at me in a game of "Gotcha!" But I have learned to see these episodes as opportunities to pose more substantive questions to the audience: Who gets to speak for a religious tradition—its practitioners or its enemies? How do we read the sacred texts of another religious community? In the case of Islam, do we read the Qur'an with the intent of reinforcing our own biases against Muslims? Or do we approach the Qur'an with deep humility and with a sincere effort to understand how Muslims themselves read and interpret it?

If the situation were reversed, I suspect Christians would want to be given the benefit of the doubt about how they read and interpret the Bible. Imagine if I walked into a church, climbed into the pulpit, opened it to the New Testament, and read aloud to the congregation this verse from Ephesians: "Slaves, obey your earthly masters with fear and trembling" (6:5). Imagine if I then closed the book and proclaimed with absolute authority: "Gotcha! You believe in enslaving human beings! I know because I read it in your book!" My hunch is that the congregation would respond with something like: "Whoa, Todd, slow down. That's not how we understand that passage."

If I want to understand how Christians interpret this text on slavery, or any other passage, I shouldn't ask their critics or people of other religions. I should ask Christians. I should read the Bible with and alongside my Christian neighbors. What I will learn along the way is that Christians read the Bible in many different ways, and that Christians look to many different biblical texts beyond a single verse in Ephesians for meaning and inspiration.

All of this applies to Muslims as well. If I want to understand how Muslims interpret the sword verse or any other passage from the Qur'an, I should ask them. I should read the Qur'an with and alongside my Muslim neighbors and try to see Islam's most sacred text through their eyes. As with Christians, what I will discover is that Muslims read their scriptures in diverse ways and look to a whole host of passages beyond the sword verse for guidance in their lives of faith.

None of this is an effort to dismiss outside perspectives on Islam or to silence criticisms of Muslim communities out of hand. If critical conversations follow, so be it, so long as these conversations move past stereotypes and reflect a sincere effort on our part to allow Muslims to define themselves.

Compare Like with Like

The second rule is never to take the worst examples in another religion and compare them to the best examples in ours. Again, this is easier said than done. Stendahl once remarked that most of us are narcissistic when it comes to our own religion. We think of it at its best while only noticing the flaws and failures of other religions.

The temptation to look to our best and compare it to their worst is particularly strong when it comes to examples of peace and violence. Christianity, we might argue, has nonviolent peacemakers such as Martin Luther King Jr. and Mother Teresa, or humanitarian organizations such as the Salvation Army. Islam, on the other hand, gives us terrorists such as Osama bin Laden or ruthless organizations such as ISIS.

I encounter these types of comparisons quite frequently, but they are patently unfair and unethical. They reflect deliberate attempts to cast Islam in the worst light possible while presenting Christianity in the best light possible. In doing so, they shield us from the truth. Both religions have their share of villains and scoundrels, of injustices and mass atrocities. Both also have their share of heroes and role models, of social justice and peacemaking movements. If our goal is to be fair and honest in our efforts to understand Islam, we must compare apples to apples, like with like.

If Christians want to know whether Islam has its own Martin Luther King, the answer is not to whip out a Who's Who list of Muslim extremists and terrorists but to identify and lift up examples of Muslims who are engaged in nonviolent peacemaking and social justice work. Granted, many of us may not know who these figures are off the top of our heads, but that's why we must do our homework and educate ourselves about the extraordinary women and men whose contributions to peace and the common good arise not in spite of Islam but because of it.

For those readers who don't even know where to start on this homework assignment, here's some help. We can begin with Muslims who are recent Nobel Peace Prize winners. Muhammad Yunus, an economist from Bangladesh, won the prize in 2006 for developing a system of financial lending to the poor, and particularly poor women, known as microfinancing. The system was eventually institutionalized when Yunus created the Grameen Bank. Yunus argued the bank reflected the true spirit of Islamic finance since Islam held a deep concern for the exploitation of the poor for financial profit. The Grameen Bank avoided such exploitation because poor borrowers owned the bank and thus loaned money to themselves.

Tawakkol Karman, a journalist and the cofounder of Women Journalists without Chains, won the prize in 2011 for her efforts before and during the Arab Spring to promote democracy and women's right in her native Yemen. She was the first Arab woman to win the prize. Karman opened her acceptance speech in Oslo with the *basmala*, the phrase that begins almost every surah, or chapter, in the Qur'an: "In the name of God the Compassionate the Merciful!" She went on to cite the Qur'an as justification for her efforts to create a more peaceful Yemen and Middle East, including the verse: "O ye who believe, enter ye into the peace, once and all" (Q. 2:208).[1]

At thirty-two, Karman was the youngest person ever to win the Nobel Peace Prize—that is, until seventeen-year-old Malala Yousafzai won the prize three years later. Yousafzai, who survived an assassination attempt by Taliban gunmen in her native Pakistan in 2012, was awarded the prize for the work that made her a Taliban target—fighting for the right of girls to receive an education. Like Karman, she began her speech with the *basmala* and went on to note the ways Islam has inspired her work for peace and education. This includes the Prophet Muhammad's injunction not to harm others, the Qur'anic prohibition against murder, and the first command given by God to Muhammad, the command to read (*iqra*).[2]

Plenty of Muslim peacemakers beyond Nobel Peace Prize winners are finding inspiration in Islam to promote justice and the common good. This includes individuals like Sakena Yacoobi, who founded the Afghan Institute of Learning (AIL) in 1995, around the same time that the Taliban was coming to power. Under Yacoobi's leadership, AIL created dozens of underground home schools for girls and women and has continued to establish schools and health clinics after the Taliban's fall. Yacoobi appeals to Islam's teachings on social justice and its commands to protect the poor and marginalized as inspiration for her work. Her educational approach relies specifically on the Qur'an. She teaches women to study the Qur'an analytically and helps them understand Qur'anic principles on gender equality.

A Muslim peacemaker who has been a significant influence in my own interfaith work is Eboo Patel, founder and president of the Interfaith Youth Core (IFYC) in Chicago and the author of the foreword to this book. Patel believes religions should be viewed not as barriers for separating people but as bridges for connecting people. Much of his work has focused on interfaith cooperation on college and university campuses, but his influence extends well beyond higher education.

Patel's work is driven by his experience as an American Muslim and the challenges of navigating the United States' diverse religious landscape. It's also driven by his conviction that Islam at its core promotes compassion through *taqwa*. Patel translates this Qur'anic term as "God consciousness" or "inner torch," describing it as "the writing of God on our souls" that orients us to do what is right and to engage others with mercy.[3]

Patel, Yunus, Karman, Yousafzai, and Yacoobi are only the tip of the iceberg. There are many more Muslims throughout the world who engage in acts of mercy and compassion, who labor for peace and promote social justice, and who do so because of the inspiration they find within Islam. We will not often see their stories on CNN or the BBC or read about them in the *New York Times*, but their work is just as important and vital for peacemaking. All of these individuals represent the best of Islam. And it's the best of Islam that deserves much more of our attention as we foster friendships with and respect for our Muslim neighbors.

Develop "Holy Envy"

The final rule is to cultivate a sense of "holy envy" toward other religions. The idea is to discover some element within them that evokes beauty or a sense of awe. Stendahl first articulated this rule in the context of responding to the controversial Mormon practice of baptizing the dead. Mormons believe vicarious baptisms of the deceased enable those who were not Mormons during their lifetime an opportunity to gain salvation even in death.

While the ritual attracts controversy among non-Mormons, particularly in instances in which Holocaust victims such as Anne Frank have been baptized posthumously, Stendahl is held in great esteem among Mormons for admiring the underlying spirit of the practice. "We Lutherans do nothing for our dead," Stendahl once lamented. Mormons, however, engage in rituals that keep them connected to their deceased ancestors and forbears. "It's a beautiful thing," Stendahl said. "I could think of myself as taking part in such an act, extending the blessings that have come to me in and through Jesus Christ. That's a beautiful way of letting the eternal mix into the temporal—which, in a way, is what Christianity is about."[4]

We can look to two former US presidents to help us understand what "holy envy" of Islam might look like. During a 2002 Eid al-Fitr dinner at the White House, President Bush expressed admiration for how the practice of fasting during Ramadan inspires Muslims "to refocus their minds and faith and redirect their hearts to charity." Fasting propels Muslims beyond their own immediate needs to show mercy and compassion to the poor.[5] In 2007, Barack Obama, then a presidential candidate, told *New York Times* columnist Nicholas Kristof the Islamic call to prayer is "one of the prettiest sounds on Earth at sunset."[6] Both Bush and Obama are Christians, and yet both find within Islam something that is beautiful or otherwise deeply compelling.

I have come to develop a deep appreciation for many aspects of Islam, but if I had to name one thing that inspires the most "holy envy" for me, it's the practice of five daily prayers. This was not always the case. When I first embarked on interfaith outreach to Muslims, I confess I did not hold this practice in such high esteem. I imagine my Protestant background had something to do with it, but I could not help but think of the practice as a burdensome list of "things to do." I even assumed most Muslims felt the same way, that they found the daily prayers cumbersome but were too afraid to say so out loud.

After years of developing friendships with Muslims and observing them at prayer on various occasions, I've changed my tune considerably. I now have deep admiration for the daily prayers. Part of this admiration pertains to their embodied nature. Protestant Christianity has a tendency to encourage disembodied relationships with the divine, to perpetuate a form of worship and adoration that takes place primarily in our heads. Muslims invest their whole bodies in prayer as they prostrate themselves and touch their head to the ground in submission to their Creator. It's a powerful reminder that the entire body, and not just that part of our body above the neck, is a spiritual conduit connecting us to the divine.

What I also admire is how the frequency of the prayers results in an infusion of the sacred into the secular. The most ordinary of days do not pass without Muslims regularly pausing to "plug in" to the ground of their being and recharge their spiritual batteries. The prayers provide a sacred ordering to daily life that is all too often missing from my own, particularly since I come from a tradition that typically relegates worship to a specific morning one day per week and makes other prayer "optional."

"Holy envy" is not a ploy to appropriate elements of Islam, or any other religion for that matter, and make them our own. This is not an exercise in spiritual plagiarism. But it is an opportunity to find beauty in Islam, and through this beauty, to develop an appreciative knowledge of Islam that opens the door to deeper dialogue and more meaningful relationships with our Muslim neighbors.

* * *

I began this book by raising a moral question in light of the rampant Islamophobia afflicting Western nations: How do we tell truths about our Muslim neighbors? Much of this book sheds light on our failures to uphold that ancient commandment not to bear false witness. Particularly on the topics of violence and terrorism, the temptation to implicate all Muslims and all of Islam in light of the atrocious acts committed by al-Qaeda or ISIS is difficult to resist. In the process, we perpetuate lies not only about Muslims but about ourselves and our own relationship to violence.

What I love about Stendahl's rules of interfaith understanding is that they put us on the right track when it comes to our moral commitments toward Muslims. All three rules encourage, even require, that we engage Muslims honestly and with respect for how they understand their own religion. The rules also embody the Golden Rule by inspiring us to "do to others as you would have them do to you" (Matthew 7:12).

Taken together, the rules constitute a solid foundation for interfaith etiquette that enables us to assume the best of our Muslim neighbors. They also encourage us to develop a genuine curiosity about Islam as it is understood and experienced by Muslims and to move beyond a mere repetition of caricatures and stereotypes that so often circulate among politicians and in the media. They require us to assume the role of students, with Muslims as our teachers and guides when it comes to understanding Islam as a lived religion.

With greater interfaith understanding comes greater empathy. That's something we need now more than ever. If our pluralistic societies have any hope of surviving, let alone thriving, in such divisive times, we will need a revolution of empathy. In the case of our Muslim neighbors, we will need to imagine ourselves in their shoes when it comes to the violence carried out in the name of Islam by extremists, to try and understand their frustrations when they are presumed guilty due to the crimes of others. More broadly, we will need to take more time to learn how Muslims read and interpret their own texts, live out their own traditions, and tell their own stories.

Only then will we know what it means to tell truths about Muslims. Only then will we be able to love our Muslim neighbors as ourselves. Only then will we have the capacity to tap into the riches and wisdom that Muslims offer as we collectively work for a more peaceful, prosperous world.

Notes

1. Tawakkol Karman, "Nobel Lecture," December 10, 2011, PDF, http://tinyurl.com/ydfezuuf. The English translation of Q. 2:208 is the one used in Karman's original speech.
2. Malala Yousafzai, "Nobel Lecture," December 10, 2014, PDF, http://tinyurl.com/y8d7mtow.
3. Eboo Patel, *Acts of Faith: The Story of an American Muslim, the Struggle for the Soul of a Generation* (Boston: Beacon, 2010), 111; Eboo Patel, "Standing Your Sacred Ground," 2013 Ware Lecture, Unitarian Universalist Association, http://tinyurl.com/y848ykka.
4. Daniel Peterson, "Defending the Faith: A Lutheran Bishop's Perspective on Mormon Baptism for the Dead," *Deseret News*, February 22, 2012, http://tinyurl.com/y7ofvh54.

5. George W. Bush, "Remarks by the President on Eid Al-Fitr," White House Archives, December 5, 2002, http://tinyurl.com/y7qmxhs3.

6. Nicholas Kristof, "Obama: Man of the World," *New York Times*, March 6, 2007, http://tinyurl.com/93ajtfg.

Suggested Further Reading

Ahmed, Akbar. *Journey into Europe: Islam, Immigration, and Identity*. Washington, DC: Brookings Institution Press, 2018.

Arjana, Sophia Rose. *Muslims in the Western Imagination*. New York: Oxford University Press, 2015.

Armstrong, Karen. *Muhammad: A Prophet for Our Time*. New York: HarperOne, 2007.

Aslan, Reza. *No God but God: The Origins, Evolution, and Future of Islam*. New York: Random House, 2011.

Bail, Christopher. *Terrified: How Anti-Muslim Fringe Organizations Became Mainstream*. Princeton: Princeton University Press, 2015.

Bayoumi, Moustafa. *This Muslim American Life: Dispatches from the War on Terror*. New York: New York University Press, 2015.

Beydoun, Khaled A. *American Islamophobia: Understanding the Roots and Rise of Fear*. Oakland: University of California Press, 2018.

Curtis, Edward E. *Muslims in America: A Short History*. New York: Oxford University Press, 2009.

———, ed. *The Practice of Islam in America: An Introduction*. New York: New York University Press, 2017.

Esposito, John L. *What Everyone Needs to Know about Islam.* New York: Oxford University Press, 2011.

Fekete, Liz. *A Suitable Enemy: Racism, Migration and Islamophobia in Europe.* London: Pluto, 2009.

Green, Todd H. *The Fear of Islam: An Introduction to Islamophobia in the West.* Minneapolis: Fortress Press, 2015.

Grewal, Zareena. *Islam Is a Foreign Country: American Muslims and the Global Crisis of Authority.* New York: New York University Press, 2014.

Hussain, Amir. *Muslims and the Making of America.* Waco, TX: Baylor University Press, 2016.

Iftikhar, Arsalan. *Scapegoats: How Islamophobia Helps Our Enemies and Threatens Our Freedoms.* New York: Hot Books, 2016.

Iyer, Deepa. *We Too Sing America: South Asian, Arab, Muslim, and Sikh Immigrants Shape Our Multiracial Future.* New York: New Press, 2017.

Kaltner, John. *Islam: What Non-Muslims Should Know.* Minneapolis: Fortress Press, 2016.

Kumar, Deepa. *Islamophobia and the Politics of Empire.* Chicago: Haymarket, 2012.

Kundnani, Arun. *The Muslims Are Coming: Islamophobia, Extremism, and the Domestic War on Terror.* London: Verso, 2014.

Kurzman, Charles. *The Missing Martyrs: Why There Are So Few Muslim Terrorists.* New York: Oxford University Press, 2011.

Lean, Nathan. *The Islamophobia Industry: How the Right Manufactures Hatred of Muslims.* London: Pluto, 2017.

Love, Erik. *Islamophobia and Racism in America.* New York: New York University Press, 2017.

Mamdani, Mahmood. *Good Muslim, Bad Muslim: America, the Cold War, and the Roots of Terror.* New York: Pantheon, 2004.

Mattson, Ingrid. *The Story of the Qur'an: Its History and Place in Muslim Life.* Chichester, UK: Wiley-Blackwell, 2013.

Nasr, Seyyed Hossein. *The Study Quran: A New Translation and Commentary.* New York: HarperOne, 2015.

Patel, Eboo. *Sacred Ground: Pluralism, Prejudice, and the Promise of America.* Boston: Beacon, 2012.

Power, Carla. *If the Oceans Were Ink: An Unlikely Friendship and a Journey to the Heart of the Quran.* New York: Holt Paperbacks, 2015.

Ramadan, Tariq. *Western Muslims and the Future of Islam.* New York: Oxford University Press, 2004.

Safi, Omid. *Memories of Muhammad: Why the Prophet Matters.* New York: HarperOne, 2009.

Said, Edward W. *Covering Islam: How the Media and the Experts Determine How We See the Rest of the World.* New York: Vintage, 1997.

Saunders, Doug. *The Myth of the Muslim Tide: Do Immigrants Threaten the West?* New York: Vintage, 2012.

Sonn, Tamara. *Is Islam an Enemy of the West?* Cambridge, UK: Polity, 2016.

———. *Islam: History, Religion, and Politics.* Malden, MA: Wiley-Blackwell, 2015.

Index

9/11 attacks, 7, 8, 15–16, 19,
20, 27, 29, 31, 33, 34, 42,
51, 52, 55, 77, 78, 84, 87,
88, 90, 109, 119–20
9/11 Memorial Museum,
119–20, 121
16th Street Baptist Church
(1963 Birmingham bomb-
ing), 129

Abaaoud, Abdelhamid, 88
Abbott, Lyman, 107–8
Abedin, Huma, 74
Abedi, Salman, 89
Abu Ghraib, 136
Abu Omar, 35
*A Common Word between Us
and You*, 65
Afghanistan. *See* Operation
Enduring Freedom

Afsaruddin, Asma, 57
Ahmed, Mohammed, 14–15
al-Awlaki, Anwar 88
al-Baghdadi, Abu Bakr. *See
Letter to Baghdadi*
Albania, 77, 79
Algerian War, 134
Ali, Kecia, 123
al-Qaradawi, Yusuf, 52
al-Qaeda, xxiv, xxv, xxvi, 7, 9,
11, 17, 51, 56, 68, 77, 79,
88, 154, 177
al-Shehhi, Marwan, 8–9
al-Yaqoubi, Muhammad,
54–55, 58, 62, 66
Amalekites, 147
American-Arab Anti-Dis-
crimination Committee,
28

American Civil Liberties
Union, 28, 109
American Jewish Committee,
3
Amman Message, 53
Amnesty International, 136
Anabaptists, 113–14
anti-Semitism, 4, 105, 111–12,
149–53
Appleton, Samuel, 147
Arab American Police Association (Chicago), 85
Arab League, 53
Arlington National Cemetery,
80
Armed Forces Muslim Association (UK), 83
Armenian genocide, 153
Association of Muslim Police
(UK), 86
Atomic bombings of Japan,
143, 154–57
Atran, Scott, 8–10, 11
Atta, Mohamed, 8–9
Aussaresses, Paul, 134
Azerbaijan, 79

Bachmann, Michele, 74
Bahrain, 77
Baldwin, James, 103
Bangladesh, 77, 171

ban, Muslim, 26, 40–42, 82
Bannon, Steve, 75, 131–32
Barman Declaration, 152
basmala, 172
Battle of Badr, 59
Battle of Horseshoe Bend,
141–42
Battle of Khaybar, 66
BBC, 15, 174
Belaroui, Amina, 83
Belaroui, Majda, 83
Belgium, 7, 113
Benton, Thomas Hart, 148
Berlin Christmas market
attack (2016), 3, 4
bin al-Shibh, Ramzi, 8–9
bin Laden, Osama, 7, 170
bin Zayd, Osama, 61
Black Lives Matter, 130–31
black sites (CIA), 35, 120, 136
Boko Haram, 61, 68
Bonhoeffer, Dietrich, 152
Bosnia and Herzegovina, 79
Bosnian genocide, 153–54
Breivik, Anders Behring, 159
Britain, 12, 14, 29–30, 32, 82,
83, 85–86, 87, 89, 134,
152, 163
Brown, Michael, 130
Brussels attack (2016), 39, 60,
87, 90

Bryant, Carolyn, 129
Bush, George W., 27–28, 29,
   42, 109, 154, 175

CAGE, 32
Cain, Herman, 38
California Gold Rush, 145
Calvin, John, 114
Cameron, David, 86
Carson, André, 75
Carson, Ben, 38–39
Charlie Hebdo attack (2015).
   See Paris, *Charlie Hebdo*
   attack (2015)
Charleston church shooting
   (2015), 50, 121, 130
Charlottesville white
   supremacist rally (2017),
   121, 130, 132
Charter of Medina, 67, 91,
   132
Chivington, John, 145
CIA, 10, 34–35, 84–85, 92,
   120, 134–37
Civilization Fund Act (1819),
   146
Civil War (US), 81, 107, 123
Clinton, Hillary, 37, 74
Cohen, Roger, xxiv

Columbus, Christopher, 142,
   144
Combating Terrorism Center,
   16–17
Comey, James, 87
Cone, James, 127
Confederate monuments, 121
Confessing Church, 152
Constitutional Convention
   (1787), 123–24
conversos, 111–12
Council on American-Islamic
   Relations (CAIR), 59, 90
Countering Violent Extrem-
   ism (CVE), 29–33
CNN, xxiv, 13, 15, 38
Creek Confederacy, 141–42
Crusades, 100, 103–6
Cruz, Ted, 39–40, 75
Cushing, Caleb, 148

database, Muslim, 27, 40
Davis, Jefferson, 122
De Blasio, Bill, 40
Department of Defense
   (DOD), 81
Department of Homeland
   Security (DHS), 28
Department of Justice (DOJ),
   33–34

deportations and detentions, 33–35

Didsbury Mosque (UK), 89

Douglass, Frederick, 125

Duke, David, 132

Egypt, xiii, 35, 78, 79

Eisenhower, Dwight D., 155

Ellison, Keith, 75

English Civil War, 105

Equal Justice Initiative, 121

Erdoğan, Recep Tayyip, xxv

Europol, 18

Euskadi Ta Askatasuna, 19

Fallujah, 79

Falwell, Jerry, 109

FBI, 12, 15, 17, 31–32, 85, 87, 88–89, 92

Ferdinand of Aragon, 111

Foley, James, 54

Fox News, xxiv

France, 7, 33, 36–37, 83, 84, 86, 106, 114, 133

Francis, Pope, xxv

François, Didier, 13

Frank, Anne, 174

Gabriel, Brigitte, 74

Gaffney, Frank, 74, 75, 167

Garner, Eric, 130

Geller, Pamela, 74, 167

genocide, 101, 142, 143–54

German Christians, 151

Germany, 3, 4, 35, 105, 108, 113, 114, 133, 149, 152

Gettysburg College, 163–65

Gingrich, Newt, 38

Global Terrorism Database, 19–20

Gore, Al, 42

Gouge, William, 105

Gregory IX, Pope, 110

Guantanamo Bay, 136

Hamas, xxiv, 7

Hamburg cell, 9

Hannity, Sean, xxiv

Hashmi, Jabron, 83

Hashmi, Zeeshan, 83

Heschel, Abraham Joshua, xv

Hezbollah, 7

Hiroshima. *See* Atomic bombings of Japan

Hiroshima Peace Memorial Museum, 156–57

Hirsi Ali, Ayaan, xxiii, 5

Hitler, Adolf, 149, 151

Holder, Eric, 87

Hollande, François, 86

Holocaust, 149–53, 159. *See also* genocide

holy envy, 174–76
holy war, 102, 103–10, 116.
 See also Crusades
Huguenots, 114
Human Rights Watch, 32
Hussain, Shahed, 31, 32
Hussein, Saddam, 78, 154

ibn Ali, Hussain, 59
ID cards, Muslim, 25
Igram, Abdullah, 81
Indian Removal Act (1830),
 146–47
Inquisition: medieval, 100,
 102, 110–11, 116; Spanish,
 100, 102, 111–13, 116
International Union of Mus-
 lim Scholars, 52
Iran, xvi, 154
Iraq, 7, 9, 13, 63, 82, 110, 136,
 143; Operation Iraqi Free-
 dom, 10–11, 77–80, 82,
 83, 93, 120, 154
Irish Republican Army, 19
Isabella of Castile, 111
Islamic Circle of North
 America, 59
Islamic Society of North
 America, 59
Israeli-Palestinian conflict, 7
ISIS, xviii, xxiv, xxvi, xxvii, 5,

7–11, 13–15, 17–18,
 49–68, 79, 85, 87, 93,
 100–101, 102, 110, 122,
 132–33, 143, 154, 156,
 170, 177
Italy, 35

Jackson, Andrew, 141–42
Jackson, Stonewall, 122
Japan, 144. *See also* Atomic
 bombings of Japan
Japanese internment camps,
 155–56
Jarrah, Ziad, 8–9
Jesus, 58, 99, 124, 127, 151,
 174
jihad, 55–57
Jim Crow era, 100, 121–22,
 128–29, 131
Jindal, Bobby, 101
Johnson, William, 131
Jordan, 53, 58, 77, 78, 79, 132

Karman, Tawakkol, 171–72
Kerry, John, 143
Khan, Abdool Rahman, 59
Khan, Ghazala, 80
Khan, Humayun, 79–81
Khan, Khizr, 80
King, Martin Luther, 75–76,
 129, 130, 170, 171

King Phillip's War, 106
KKK, 131, 132
Kocho (Iraq), 63
Kristof, Nicholas, 175
Kurzman, Charles, 87
Kuwait, 78, 79

Leahy, William, 155
Lebanon, 7
Lee, Robert E., 122
Leiter, Michael, 85
Letter to Baghdadi, 54, 56,
    60–61, 62, 64, 65
Le Pen, Marine, 36–37
Lest We Forget Museum of
    Slavery, 121
Lincoln, Abraham, 107
London: London bombings
    (2005), 29, 51; Westmin-
    ster bridge attack (2017), 3
Louis Philippe I, 106
Luther College, 25–27
Luther, Martin, 113, 150–51
lynchings, 121–22, 126–28

MacArthur, Douglas, 155
Madrid train bombings
    (2004), 20, 51
Maher, Bill, xxiii
Malaysia, 79
Malik, Mohammed, 88–89

Malleus Maleficarum, 115–16
Manchester attack (2017), 89,
    91
Manifest Destiny, 147–48
Marrakesh Declaration, 66–67
Martins, Olly, 86
Martin, Trayvon, 130
Mary I, 114
Mateen, Omar, 87, 88–89
Mather, Cotton, 147
Matthews, Chris, 157
Mau Mau Uprising, 134
May, Theresa, 87, 163
Mazzini, Giuseppe, 105
McCaskill, Claire, 17–18
McVeigh, Timothy, 15
Meet the Press, 85
Merabet, Ahmed, 86
MI5, 12–13, 14
MI6, 92
Mitchell, Andrea, 101
Moore, Russell, 101
moriscos, 112
Mormons, 174
Morrison, Toni, 158
Moses, 58
Mosul, 79
Mother Teresa, 170
Muhammad (Prophet), 53, 54,
    55, 56, 58, 59, 60, 64, 65,
    66, 67, 91, 163, 172

Muslim Brotherhood, 74–75, 167

Muslim Public Affairs Council, 59, 63, 88

Muslims Condemn, 51

Muslims for Life, 90

Muslims United: for London, 90; for San Bernardino Families, 90; for the Victims of Pulse Shooting, 90

Nagasaki. *See* Atomic bombings of Japan

National Association of Muslim Police (UK), 85–86

National Prayer Breakfast, 99–101

National Front (France), 36

National Religious Campaign against Torture, 59

National Union of Teachers (UK), 32

Native American genocide, 144–49. *See also* genocide

NATO, 77

Netherlands, 36–37, 113

Newburgh terrorist plot (2009), 31–32

New York Times, xxiv, 174, 175

Nice terrorist attack (2016), 83

Niemöller, Martin, 152, 153

Nobel Peace Prize, xiii, 171–73

No One Left Behind, 82

North Korea, 154

Norway attacks (2011)

NYPD, 30–31, 40, 85, 130

Obama, Barack, xvii, xxiv–xxv, 28, 29, 37–38, 80, 87, 100–101, 132, 136, 156–57, 175

Oklahoma City bombing (1995), 15

Old Slave Mart Museum, 121

Operation Absconder, 34

Operation Enduring Freedom, 76–78, 83, 120

Orlando nightclub shooting (2016), 87, 88–89, 90

Ottoman Empire. *See* Turkey

Page, Wade Michael, 159

Palin, Sarah, 157

Pape, Robert, 6–8, 11

Pakistan, 77, 100

Paris: *Charlie Hebdo* attack (2015), 3, 33, 51, 60, 86, 88; kosher supermarket

attack (2015), 3, 4;
November 2015 attack, 3,
33, 40, 51, 60, 90
Party for Freedom (Nether-
lands), 36
Patel, Eboo, xii–xiii, xv–xviii,
173
People of the Book, 64–67
Pequot War, 145
Philip III, 112
Phoenix Program, 134–35
Pius XI, Pope, 152
Pius XII, Pope, 152–53
Poland, 35
Portland train attack (2017),
91
Powell, Colin, 37
Prevent (UK), 29–30, 32
Purinton, Adam, xvi

Qadri, Muhammad Tahir, 53,
63, 65, 66
Qatar, 78
Qur'an, 13, 37, 52, 56, 60, 62,
63–64, 65, 66, 90, 91,
168–69, 172, 173

registration programs:
NSEERS (National Secu-
rity Entry-Exist Registra-
tion System), 27–29, 34;
Trump proposal, 25, 27.
See also database, Muslim
Reformation, 113–14
Republican National Com-
mittee, 148
Revolutionary War, 81, 106–7
Rice, Tamir, 130
Roma, 149
Romania, 35
Roof, Dylann, 50
Roosevelt, Franklin, 108,
155–56

Sachedina, Abdulaziz, 57
Sageman, Marc, 10–11
Saladin, 104
Salvation Army, 170
San Bernardino attack (2015),
40–41, 90
Sand Creek Massacre, 145
Sarsour, Linda, 57
Sarwar, Yusuf, 14–15
Saudi Arabia, 78
School of the Americas,
135–36
Scott, Walter, 106
Senate Intelligence Commit-
tee (US): Report on Tor-
ture (2014), 35, 136
Servetus, Michael, 114
Shahabuddin, Syed, 56

Shahada, 60–61
Sharia, 13, 14, 38–39, 62;
   anti-Sharia bills, 39
Shekau, Abubakr, 61
Sikhs, 26
Sixtus IV, Pope, 111
slavery: in the United States,
   100, 121–22, 122–26, 131;
   ISIS, 61–63
Somali American Police Asso-
   ciation (Minneapolis), 85
Sotloff, Steven, 54
Spencer, Robert, 74, 163–65,
   167
State Department (US), viii,
   73–75
Stendahl, Krister, 165–66,
   170, 174–75
surveillance, 29–33
Sweden, xv
Smithsonian, 156
Switzerland, 113, 114
Syria, 9, 11, 13, 14, 54, 79, 81,
   110, 143

takfir, 60–61
Taliban, 77, 79, 83, 172–73
Tamil Tigers, 6–7
taqiyya, 39
taqwa, 173
Taylor, Charles, xvii

Thornwell, James Henley, 125
Thirty Years' War, 105
Till, Emmett, 129
Todd, Chuck, 85
torture, 34–35, 101, 110,
   112–13, 114, 120, 132–38
Trail of Tears, 146–47
Travel ban. *See* ban, Muslim
Triangle Center on Terrorism
   and Homeland Security,
   16, 17
Truman, Harry S., 154–56
Trump, Donald, xi, xv, xvi, 4,
   5, 26, 27, 28, 38, 29,
   40–42, 49, 74–75, 80, 82,
   85, 87, 131–32, 157
Turkey, xxv, 77, 78, 79, 112,
   153

United Arab Emirates, 77, 79
United Nations, 11, 13, 133,
   146
Urban II, Pope, 104

Vietnam War, 81, 134–35
Vorwerk, Dietrich, 108

Washington, George, 107
Washington, Jesse (1916
   lynching), 127–28
Washington Post, 85, 130

white supremacy, xxvi, 17–18, 121–32

Wilders, Geert, 36–37

Wilhelm II, 108

Wilson, Lydia, 13

witch trials, 114–16

Wofford College, xxi–xxii

Wood, Graeme, 5

Wordsworth, William, 106

World Trade Center, 119–20

World War I, 81, 82, 107–8

World War II, 38, 81, 83, 108, 133, 134, 143, 149–53

Wray, Chris, 17

Yacoobi, Sakena, 172–73

Yazidis, 62, 63, 64, 100, 110, 122, 143

Young Americans for Freedom, 163–64

Yousafzai, Malala, 172

Yuki, 145–46

Yunus, Muhammad, 171

Yusuf, Hamza, 53

Zimmerman, George, 130